ISBN: 978-0-9894338-2-2
Cover Design: Jenna Stanbrough
Book Layout: Bethany Stanbrough
Front Cover Photos: Spencer Allen and Pretty Sporty/Cheryl Treworgy

Roho Publishing
4040 Graphic Arts Road
Emporia, KS 66801

www.rohopublishing.com

About Roho Publishing

When Kip Keino defeated Jim Ryun in the 1968 Olympic Games at 1500 meters he credited the win to "Roho." Roho is the Swahili word for spirit demonstrated through extraordinary strength and courage. The type of courage and strength that can be summoned up from deep within that will allow you to meet your goals and overcome the challenges in life. Roho Publishing focuses on the spirit of sport and is designed to inspire, encourage, motivate and teach valuable life lessons.

Dedication

To all coaches who work with young people on a daily basis and make a difference. You make a difference in developing not only the physical components, but also the hearts and minds of athletes.

Acknowledgements

Thanks to my parents, who instilled integrity, a strong work ethic, perseverance and pride.

I would like to acknowledge my daughters, Bethany, Leslie and Jenna. Fortunately, Bethany and Jenna majored in journalism and mass media, respectively, and have been an integral part of editing and developing this book.

I want to thank my wonderful wife who has supported me in all my projects. Her support has been an inspiration.

I would like to thank all the coaches I have had over the years who made a difference in my life. I would also like to thank the athletes whom I have had the privilege to coach over the years. Each of these individuals have taught me much about the qualities to be successful in life—good character, integrity, a strong work ethic, dedication, and perseverance.

Introduction

The most important thing in the Olympic Games is not to win but to take part, just as the most important thing in life is not the triumph but the struggle. The essential thing is not to have conquered but to have fought well. – The Olympic Creed

Motivational Moments in Women's Track and Field is designed to inspire, encourage, motivate, and teach us valuable life lessons. The stories are written for those who are currently competing, coaching, have participated in track and field, or are simply a track and field or sports fan. The questions at the end of the stories are designed to challenge, teach and enable you to grow as you apply these principles to athletics and to the bigger game of life.

All of the athletes are ordinary people who used extraordinary desire to accomplish extraordinary things. Each athlete began simply with a dream, which developed into a belief in themselves. They personify the Olympic philosophy – "there are no great people, rather there are great challenges that ordinary people are forced to meet." Their stories offer hope that we can dream and reach beyond our perceived abilities and achieve personal satisfaction.

The stories are rich in history and designed to be read in a few minutes. The stories pay honor to all the young men and women who enter the arena, who make the attempt, and pursue excellence. These stories of great athletes teach us how to eliminate negative thinking, to focus our attention on what is important, and how to overcome obstacles to reach our goals.

Athletes throughout the past century have entered the competitive arena and competed with honor. Although not all athletes are fortunate to catch an Olympic star, all athletes can valiantly reach for the heavens. Their stories of inspiration should be read and remembered. For it has been written, *"The honor should not alone go to those who have not fallen; rather all honor to those who fall and rise again."*

This book was designed to be enjoyed by anyone with an interest in track and field, but the author, who has over thirty years of experience in coaching track and field at both the high school and collegiate level, wrote this book especially with track and field coaches in mind. If you are a coach, you are encouraged to use these stories to motivate and inspire your athletes. Coaching is one of the most influential professions in our society. Coaches work with young people on a daily basis and have a tremendous opportunity to make a difference. Athletics is about more than just playing a game. It is the responsibility of the coach to develop not only the physical component, but to develop the heart and mind of each athlete they coach.

Our young people need strong role models. The athletes profiled display the drive, motivation, and dedication to train for years to reach a goal. Their stories teach the values of self-discipline, responsibility, accountability, and loyalty. They demonstrate the qualities necessary to be successful in life—good character, integrity, a strong work ethic, dedication, and perseverance. You're bound to find motivation and encouragement, no matter what your experience or relationship to track and field. Hopefully you receive pleasure and inspiration from these pages, just as you have found pleasure and inspiration from the greatest sport in the world—track and field.

Using the Questions for Thought in a Coaching Environment

The short stories are designed to be read in a few minutes and can be posted on bulletin boards or distributed for group discussions. The questions at the end of each story are designed to inspire thinking, encourage, challenge and impart a learning lesson.

The principles embedded in the stories can be applied to athletics, but more importantly to the bigger game of life. Rather than hoping athletes can be gaining positive lessons from the athletic experience, the coach can be proactive by educating athletes through a story and its applications to athletics and life.

There are many ways the questions can be used with an athletic team. Here are ten suggestions.

1. Post on bulletin board for all to read.

2. Distribute event specific stories to athletes.

3. Coach reads story. Group discussion takes place.

4. Athletes are assigned to read stories to team. Group discussion takes place after story is read.

5. Athletes read story within small group. Small group discussion takes place after story is read.

6. Team discusses questions during warm-up activity or drill.

7. Stories can be read during a break in practice.

8. Questions can be discussed during a break in practice.

9. Reading of story and discussion on stories can take place after practice.

10. Athletes can be given a story to help motivate them when injured or performance is sub-par.

Sample questions from Lolo Jones story:

1. Lolo overcame a difficult childhood to be successful. How can you use her story for motivation?

2. Lolo thought about giving up track at one time, but her heart was still in it. How does heart factor into success?

3. Lolo overcame the odds to return to the Olympics. What odds have you overcome?

Index

Index

Page	Last Name	First Name	Event	Story Overview
38	Harper	Dawn	Hurdles	Surprise gold medal winner after she overcame knee injury
39	Harrison	Queen	Hurdles	Had to hurdle fallen athlete in her lane to become youngest member of U.S. team
40	Hayes	Joanna	Hurdles	Returned from injuries to win Olympic gold
41	Holmes	Kelly	Mid-Distance	Pressure was so great, she cut herself and considered suicide
42	Jennings	Lynn	Distance	Won more U.S cross country titles than any other woman
43	Joyner-Kersee	Jackie	Multi-Events	Overcame a challenging childhood, asthma, and injuries to become greatest female athlete
44	Jones	Lolo	Hurdles	Overcame disappointment of Olympic hurdling and injury to make U.S. team
45	Larrieu Smith	Francie	Distance	Made five Olympic teams from 1500 meters to the marathon
46	Manning-Mims	Madeline	Distance	Made four Olympic teams, despite her event, the 400 meters, not being contested in the Olympics
47	Miles-Clark	Jearl	Mid-Distance	Made five Olympic teams
48	Mutola	Maria	Distance	Left her home country to seek better training and competed in six Olympics
49	Pickett/Stokes	Tidye/Louise	Sprints/Hurdles	First African American female athletes in Olympics
50	Ottey	Merlene	Sprints	Made eight Olympic teams
51	Quirot	Anna	Distance	Country boycotted two Olympic Games, came back from severe burns in explosion
52	Radcliffe	Paula	Distance	Overcame injuries
53	Richards-Ross	Sanya	Sprints	Deals with Behcet's syndrome
54	Ritter	Louis	Jumps	Overcame rheumatic fever and injuries to win Olympics despite being an underdog
55	Robinson	Betty	Sprints	Badly injured in plane crash, came back to win gold
56	Rudolph	Wilma	Sprints	Had polio as a child and was told she would never walk again, won three gold medals
57	Runyan	Marla	Distance	First legally blind athlete to compete in Olympic Games
58	Schmidt	Kate	Throws	Denied an opportunity to compete because of Olympic boycott when she was at her best
59	Smith-Carson	Janelle	Sprints	Overcame lack of women's track programs to set American record at 400 meters
60	Stephens	Helen	Sprints/Throws	Ran over 100 races and never lost
61	Switzer	Katherine	Distance	Overcame discrimination against womens running
62	Torrence	Gwen	Sprints	Grew up in poverty and around drugs
63	Vlasic	Blanka	Jumps	Competed in her first Olympics at age 16
64	Willliams	Lauryn	Sprints	Only 5-3, proved that hard work counts more than size
65	Whitbread	Fatima	Throws	Grew up in poverty and cruelty
66	White	Willye	Sprints	Came out of cotton field to make five Olympic teams

Evelyn Ashford

A Spirited Run

As Evelyn Ashford was running during physical education class in high school, the football coach pulled her aside and asked if she would race his fastest player. Evelyn won the race, and because there was no girl's track team, she joined the boy's track team. By her senior year in high school, she had won numerous state and regional track meets, racing against other girls. After a successful high school career, Evelyn went to UCLA and began training for the 1976 Montreal Olympics. As a freshman in college, she placed fifth in the 100 meters at the Montreal Olympic Games.

Her next two years in college, she won both the 100 and 200 meters in the NCAA Championships. Another two years of training and she was a world champion at 100 meters with the No. 1 ranking in the world at the age of 23. Evelyn believed she was in the prime of her career as the time neared for the 1980 Olympic Games in Moscow, U.S.S.R. When the United States boycotted the Olympic Games, Evelyn, along with dozens of other American athletes, was devastated at being denied the opportunity to compete for honors that they had dedicated their entire careers toward.

After temporarily abandoning her training, she resumed it with an eye towards the 1984 Games in Los Angeles. She set her first world record for the 100 meters, running 10.79. However, after winning her first two 100-meter races in the 1983 World Championships, she pulled her right hamstring muscle and fell in the final race. The injury stayed with her into 1984 and was still bothering her as the 1984 Olympics began. At the 1984 Summer Olympics, Evelyn won the 100 meters in a new Olympic record of 10.97 and anchored the 4x100-meter relay team to a gold medal.

Evelyn took time off to have a baby in 1985 and many thought she might retire from running. However, she proved them wrong by qualifying for her third Olympic Games in Seoul, South Korea in 1988, and she had the honor of being the U.S. flag bearer for the opening ceremonies. She finished second in the 100-meter race behind her American teammate, Florence Griffith Joyner. In the 4x100-meter relay, she again anchored her team to a gold medal.

Evelyn Ashford competed in her fourth and final Olympics in Barcelona, Spain, at the age of 35. As the oldest runner in the sprinting events, she won her fourth gold medal in the 4x100-meter relay. Evelyn's 17-year running career and four Olympic appearances are an inspiration to all young girls and women.

Questions for Thought:

1. Evelyn had early success and continued for many years. What are some keys to being a good athlete over a long period of time?

2. Because she was dependable, Evelyn anchored her relay teams. What do people depend on you for? Are you reliable?

3. Evelyn had an opportunity to win more gold medals in 1980, but because of a U.S. boycott, did not get to compete. How do you recover from major disappointments?

Iolanda Balas

The Streaker

Public Domain Photo

At the age of 12, Iolanda Balas of Romania, started high jumping and developed a modified version of the scissors technique. Iolanda set her first world record in 1956, when she cleared 5-8¾. She held the world record and was the favorite entering the 1956 Melbourne, Australia, Olympic Games. The best she could do that day was to place fifth and the winner, Millie McDaniel of the United States, broke Iolanda's world record. That would be Iolanda's last loss for more than 10 years.

Iolanda became the most dominating high jumper in history. She was the first woman to clear 6 feet, an achievement she accomplished in 1959. She solidified her reputation as unbeatable at the Rome Olympics in 1960, when she won her first gold medal, winning by an amazing margin of six inches.

Her winning streak continued day in and day out. Despite cold, rainy, and windy conditions, Iolanda continued to win. Despite multiple leg injuries she continued to amass win after win. In 1964, at the Tokyo Olympics in Japan, despite suffering from tendon and knee problems, Iolanda captured her second Olympic gold medal by jumping 6-2¾.

Iolanda was as consistent of a performer as any in history. She won 80 high jump events with leaps higher than any other woman in history had ever achieved. No high jumper, man or woman, has ever been that much better than his or her competitors. Between her loss at the 1956 Olympics and at a competition in 1966, she won a phenomenal 140 competitions in a row.

Iolanda Balas' record of 6-3¼ that she set in 1961 lasted 10 years, until jumpers began using more efficient techniques such as the straddle and Fosbury flop.

Questions for Thought:

1. Iolanda was one of the most consistent performers ever. What is the key to being consistent?

2. Iolanda's streak reached 140 straight wins. The pressure to continue her streak continued to build after each win. What are effective ways to handle pressure?

3. Once people are successful, there is a tendency to be satisfied and to stop working as hard. How do you avoid that natural tendency to stop pushing yourself?

Kim Batten

It's All About the Hurdles

Kim Batten's first sport was basketball. She began her track career as a junior in high school and won a state championship in her very first year. Kim was better known as a jumper than a hurdler in high school, where she had marks of 19-8 in the long jump, and 40-6 in the triple jump, which ranked third in the nation. She also had a best of 1:00.94 in the 400-meter hurdles. Kim attended Florida State, where she established herself as one of the finest track athletes in school history. In addition to the hurdle events, Kim starred in multiple events including the long jump, triple jump, and the 100, 200, and 400-meter dashes, as well as relays.

Her freshman year at Florida State, she competed in the 1988 Olympic Trials and was sixth in her 400-meter hurdle heat, failing to qualify for the final. She graduated in 1991 and won her first U.S. title, upsetting the United States' top hurdler, Sandra Farmer-Patrick, to win the U.S. title in 54.18.

In 1992, she competed in the U.S. Olympic Trials and improved to a fourth place finish. Despite the improvement from four years earlier, she was bitterly disappointed in narrowly missing a spot on the U.S. Olympic team.

Kim had an emergency appendectomy in 1995 just three weeks before winning at the U.S. Championships to qualify for the World Championships. Her greatest race came later that year in the 400-meter hurdle final at the World Championships. Americans Tonya Buford and Kim were both running the race of their lives. They touched down off hurdle eight, matching each other stride for stride over the last two hurdles. Kim won by a mere one-hundredth of a second. Both athletes broke the previous world record.

In 1996, she won the Olympic Trials and headed to the Olympics in Atlanta. She made a tactical mistake, stuttering before the eighth hurdle and had to settle for the Olympic silver medal.

An injury to a nerve in her foot caused Kim to miss most of the 1999 season, but she came back to finish second in the 400-meter hurdles at the 2000 Olympic Trials and placed sixth in the 2000 Olympics semifinal. Kim Batten, a six time U.S. Outdoor Champion and world record holder, retired at the end of the 2001 season.

Questions for Thought:

1. Kim barely missed an Olympic team berth in 1992, but that motivated her to work harder. What failures have you had that motivated you to work harder?

2. Besides being a great competitor, Kim was a great friend to those she competed against. Can you be a competitor as well as a friend to fellow foes?

3. Kim was a great team person in college. How would you rate yourself on a scale of 1-10 on being a team person?

Joan Benoit Samuelson

No Guts, No Glory

Joan Benoit Samuelson is one of the all-time greatest marathoners the world has ever seen. Her dedication and courageous running took her to the top of the running world, making history in the process. Joan took to long distance running to help recover from a broken leg suffered while skiing.

At Bowdoin College, she excelled in athletics for two years and then transferred to North Carolina State to focus on running, earning All-America honors. She entered the 1979 Boston Marathon as a relative unknown. She won the race in 2:35:15, taking eight minutes off the course record. She repeated that success with a record-setting victory again in 1983, taking more than two minutes off the world's best time.

In the months leading up to the 1984 U.S. Olympic Marathon Trials, Joan was hampered by a knee injury. With just 17 days to go before the Olympic Trials race, Joan visited an orthopedic surgeon, who advised her to have an arthroscopic procedure to release the plica, a small band of tissue that was causing her knee to lock. Joan took his advice, had the surgery and the day after surgery immediately got back into training, working out on a hand ergometer (moving pedals with your hands and arms). Amazingly, just 17 days later, Joan made the U.S. Olympic marathon team.

History was made at the 1984 Olympic Games hosted by Los Angeles. It was the first ever women's Olympic Marathon. Women had come a long way since 1928, when it was deemed too exhaustive for women to run over 200 meters in a race. The field included marathon legends Grete Waitz, Rosa Mota, and Ingrid Kristianson. Few of the Olympic runners knew who Joan was, so when she went to the lead early, they didn't worry about her and hung back. In the hot and smoggy conditions, the small runner with a big heart and desire continued to pound out mile after mile and won the first Olympic women's marathon in a time of 2:24:52, more than a minute ahead of her rivals.

Joan has continued to be a role model for women's running. She has written books and is a motivational speaker and a coach. She still runs competitively and for fun. At the age of 50 she ran the 2008 U.S. Olympic Marathon Trials in 2:48:08, making her the only woman to run sub-2:50 marathons over five decades.

A pioneer in women's distance running, Joan qualified for seven Olympic Marathon Trials. She is an inspiration to women and runners throughout the world that with dreams and dedication, challenging goals can be achieved.

Questions for Thought:

1. How did Joan handle her injuries?

2. Although not the race favorite, how did Joan approach the Olympic Marathon in 1984?

3. How can you run with guts to achieve the glory?

Gretel Bergmann

Betrayed

Gretel Bergmann was the daughter of a wealthy Jewish entrepreneur who quickly discovered her passion for athletics. She excelled to become Germany's national female high jump champion during the 1930s. But shortly after Adolf Hitler seized power in 1933, the harassment began. Jews were ostracized and unfairly discriminated against. Despite previously being named a member of the German Olympic team, she was no longer welcome to train at her club or with her longtime coach, and was denied the opportunity to compete.

When Gretel was 19 years old, she was sent by her parents to live in England with a goal of competing for Great Britain in the 1936 Olympic Games. After winning the 1934 British high jump championship, the Nazis ordered her to return to Germany in 1936. The United States had threatened to boycott the Olympic Games because of the persecution of Jews in Germany, and the Nazi propaganda machine needed to present a token Jew at the games. Facing threats to her family if she did not return home and compete for Germany, Gretel returned.

The training conditions back in Germany were horrible. However, Gretel overcame the adversity and tied the German and European high jump record of 5-3. Two weeks later, German sport authorities delivered a letter stating that her achievement was not good enough to represent Germany in the Olympics. Being denied the opportunity was what she described as "the worst moment of my life," because Gretel relished the opportunity to show that a Jewish girl could be as good as anybody else.

Ironically, at the same time, the United States was setting sail for the Berlin Games. The controversial Olympic boycott movement had failed, with top U.S. officials convinced that there was not mistreatment of the Jews in Germany. The gold medal in the high jump went to Hungarian Ibolya Csak who was, ironically, Jewish. The bronze went to the German "Aryan" Elfriede Kaun.

A year after the 1936 Olympic Games, Gretel immigrated to the United States and won the U.S. women's high jump and shot put championships in 1937 and the high jump title again in 1938. Gretel would eventually became a U.S. citizen. When World War II began and the Olympics scheduled to be held in 1940 and 1944 were cancelled, Gretel's Olympic dream was over. Gretel Bergmann's Olympic story is one of triumph and betrayal. Gretel was denied the opportunity to prove she was among the best.

Questions for Thought:

1. Gretel faced tremendous discrimination in her attempts to compete as an athlete. What is the greatest difficulty you have faced? How did you overcome the difficulty?

2. Athletics is a privilege to be able to participate in. How much do you appreciate the privilege to have that opportunity?

3. Gretel had no facilities to train in, yet improvised and set records. What are some ways you have improvised and have successfully overcome barriers?

Fanny Blankers-Koen

The Flying Housewife

Francina "Fanny" Blankers-Koen, a Dutch athlete, competed during a time when the sports public disregarded women's athletics. She started track and field at the age of 17, and in only her third race, she set a national record in the 800 meters. However, the 800 meters was considered too physically demanding for female contestants and had been removed from the Olympic program after 1928. So Fanny, at 18 years of age, made the Dutch team as a sprinter and high jumper. At the 1936 Berlin Olympics, she placed fifth in the high jump and ran a leg on the fifth place 4x100-meter relay team.

Her opportunity to compete in another Olympics was denied by the cancellation of the 1940 and 1944 Olympics due to World War II. Fanny managed to set world records in the sprints, hurdles, high jump, and long jump during the war years. However, training was not easy due to the war. Sport was the last thing on people's minds.

When Fanny gave birth to her first child, it was automatically assumed her career would be over, as top female athletes who were married were rare at the time, and it was considered inconceivable that a mother could be an athlete. Fanny had other plans though, and she resumed training just weeks after her son's birth, earning the nickname "The Flying Housewife." Although she held six world records at the time, many believed that a 30-year-old mother of two was too old to be an athlete and should stay home.

At the 1948 Olympics in London, her first win was the 100 meters, and she became the first Dutch athlete to win an Olympic title in track and field. She won a second gold in a tight 80-meter hurdle finish. Fanny picked up a third gold in the 200-meter dash, which was the first time the women's 200 meters had been held. In her fourth and final event, the 4x100-meter relay, Fanny was running the anchor when she received the baton in third place, some five meters behind Australia and Canada. Burning the straightaway, she passed both runners ahead of her to win gold for her country.

At age 34, she took part in her third Olympics at the 1952 Helsinki Games, but she hit a hurdle, which took her out of the race. It was her last major competition. Fanny Blankers-Koen's last moment of glory came in 1999, when the International Association of Athletics Federations (I.A.A.F.) declared her the "Female Athlete of the Century."

Questions for Thought:

1. It was once thought that most of the track and field events were too strenuous for women to compete in. How has history proven that wrong?

2. During Fanny's time, 30-years-old was deemed too old, and being a mother and an athlete was considered inconceivable. What has changed since the 1940s?

3. Although she missed two Olympics canceled due to war, Fanny was named "Female Athlete of the Century." What would it be like to miss the prime of your career?

Hassiba Boulmerka

The Constantine Gazelle

Hassiba Boulmerka was born in Constantine, Algeria. She first started running at the age of 10, focusing on middle distance events. She didn't face much competition locally, but ran her first major meet in the 1988 Olympics in Seoul. She was eliminated in the preliminary rounds in both the 800 and 1500 meters.

Hassiba continued to improve, and in 1991, she became the first African woman to win a World Championship when she sprinted to victory in the 1500 meters. Her remarkable performances were catching the attention of the world, but she faced grave dangers at home. The country was in the grip of war and some radicals thought the track was not the right place for a woman. Muslim groups in Algeria thought she showed too much of her body when racing.

In the training leading up to the Barcelona Olympics, it became too dangerous for her to train in her own country. She received death threats and fearing she could be killed at any moment, she was forced to move to Europe to train. It was an emotional time for Hassiba, as she had to leave a family she was close to, shedding many tears of sacrifice. She abandoned the people she loved, having to severe ties with them to keep them from being harmed by militants. To complicate matters even more, her father suffered a stroke and went into a coma. Hassiba remained determined, striving to reach her goal of Olympic gold.

The death threats continued as the Barcelona Olympics approached. She had police protection during her warm-up for the competition, and even had stadium police accompany her to the bathroom. In spite of all the challenges of a very tumultuous situation, she was one of the favorites for the 1500 meters gold medal at the 1992 Barcelona Olympics. In the final, she finished strong down the stretch to win the gold medal. It was Algeria's first gold medal ever at the Olympic Games.

Hassiba hadn't won a single race in 1995 going into the World Championships, but she won her second world title. That would turn out to be her last major victory. She competed at the 1996 Olympics in Atlanta, but sprained her ankle in the semifinals.

Algeria's Hassiba Boulmerka's run to victory at the Barcelona Olympics was more than just her country's first Olympic gold medal; it was a triumph for women all over the world that proved they could overcome prejudice to achieve their goals.

Questions for Thought:

1. Hassiba overcame prejudice to achieve her goals. How would you handle prejudice?

2. Hassiba had to leave her family to continue striving for her goals. What are some sacrifices you have made to reach goals?

3. Hassiba demonstrated courage and has become a role model for women all over the world. How do you define courage?

Valerie Brisco-Hooks

Dominating Doubler

Valerie Brisco-Hooks was born in Greenwood, Mississippi, and had nine brothers and sisters. She moved with her family to an urban ghetto, the Watts neighborhood of Los Angeles, before she entered elementary school. Valerie's older brother, Robert, was a star runner at Locke High School in Los Angeles. When Valerie was 14 years old, Robert and another runner were finishing a workout at the high school track when a stray bullet struck Robert, and he was killed.

Until her brother's death, Valerie was undisciplined and rebellious. The loss of her brother helped her to set personal goals and dedicate herself to achieving them. Valerie continued to excel in her track career at the collegiate level while she attended California State-Northridge. She married former Cal State-Northridge track standout Alvin Hooks, gave birth to a son, and gained 70 pounds above her competitive weight of 130.

Her husband, along with her former college coach Bobby Kersee, persuaded her that she could compete again at a world-class level and Valerie gradually got back into the best shape of her life. At the 1984 Olympic Trials, Valerie qualified to represent the United States in the individual 200 and 400-meter races and the 4x400-meter relay.

Valerie was running in her home town of Los Angeles and set high goals to win both the 200-meter and 400-meter races in the same Olympic Games, a feat no athlete had ever done. Valerie left no doubt about who was the best sprinter in the Olympics. She dominated her competition in both the 200 and 400-meter races and later capped her Olympic performance by running a leg on the United States women's victorious 4x400-meter relay team.

Valerie came back four years later and ran on the USA 4x400-meter relay team that finished second at the 1988 Olympics and set an American record.

Questions for Thought:

1. When have you set the bar high in establishing your goals?

2. After establishing a high goal, how do you achieve it?

3. If you were out of shape, how would you get back into the best shape of your life?

Earlene Brown

American Champion

Earlene Brown began her track and field career in 1956 and won the Amateur Athletic Union (A.A.U.) Championship in the shot put that same year with an American record throw of 45-0. She won the shot put at the 1956 Olympic Trials and extended her American record to 46-9½. She competed in the 1956 Olympics and set American records in both the shot put, where she finished sixth, and in the discus, where she finished fourth.

Earlene won eight A.A.U national championships in the shot put, becoming the first American to throw over 50 feet in 1958 when she was ranked No.1 in the world in the shot put. She also added three more national titles in the discus.

Earlene's greatest honor in track came during the 1960 Olympic Games in Rome when she became the only American woman ever to win an Olympic medal in the shot put. She won the bronze medal with a throw of 52-11¾. She also placed sixth in the Olympic discus with a throw of 168-3¼.

Her career continued at the 1964 Olympics, where she placed 12th in the shot put. After the 1964 Olympics, Earlene retired from track and field competition and became a star in roller derby.

Earlene Brown made history by becoming the only American woman to win a gold medal in the shot put. Her pioneering efforts have established her as one of the greatest American female throwers of all time.

Questions for Thought:

1. Earlene set an American record the first year she competed in track and field. How do you handle success?

2. Earlene is the only American woman to ever win a gold medal in the shot put. What do you believe has limited American success in the throwing events?

3. How did Earlene set the stage for future athletes?

Doris Brown Heritage

She Ran The Extra Mile

Doris Heritage faced many obstacles as a pioneer in women's distance running. Her high school banned girls from using the school track, so she joined a local running club and set a national record in the 440-yard dash. Although Doris was better at the longer distances, the longest race for women in the Olympics was the 800-meter run. So, she trained for the 800 meters and finished third at the 1960 U.S. Olympic Trials. Unfortunately, her time didn't qualify her for the Rome Olympics.

Women were originally denied participation in the modern Olympic Games when they began in 1896. They were finally granted an experimental program of five track and field events in the 1928 Olympic Games. At the end of the 800-meter run, the women were exhausted and dropped to the ground in fatigue. Olympic officials consisting entirely of men decided that races 800 meters and above were too strenuous and would cause harm to females. Therefore, the longest run competed in the Olympics from 1932 to 1956 was the 400-meter run. The 800-meter run was later added as the longest women's race in 1960.

In the 1960s, schools rarely allowed women to compete, but that began to change when Doris teamed up with Seattle Pacific's track and field coach, Ken Foreman. Doris gained an advocate in Foreman, who helped her blast through the wall that prevented women athletes from reaching their full potential.

At Seattle Pacific College, she began running with the men's team, but a broken foot kept her off the 1964 Olympic team. In 1966, she became the first woman to run a sub-5:00 mile indoors, clocking 4:52. By the following year, she began her string of five world cross country championships, the first five years in which this international competition took place. In 1968, she finished fifth in the 800 meters at the Mexico City Olympics.

By the time Congress passed Title IX in 1972, leveling the playing field of women's high school and college athletics, Doris had been running competitively for 12 years. Doris Brown Heritage was a pioneer in women's running. At one point in her career, she held every women's national and world record from 440 yards up to the mile. After her competitive career, she became an outstanding distance running coach at Seattle Pacific University and was named an assistant coach for the U.S. women's team at the 1984 Olympics and 1987 Outdoor World Championships.

Questions for Thought:

1. What obstacles did Doris have to overcome to achieve success?

2. How successful would you be if you had no track, no uniform, no team, and a lack of meets to run in? How would you overcome those barriers?

3. At one time, experts thought that women could not run 800 meters or farther without doing physical harm. How have women proved they are capable of competing in the same events men do?

Stephanie Brown-Trafton

Surprise Champion

Photo Courtesy of USATF

Stephanie Brown-Trafton was 4 years old when her mother died. She began throwing the shot put and discus in junior high school and eventually became one of the top high school throwers in the nation. Her first two years in college at Cal Poly San Luis Obispo University in California, she competed in basketball and track and field. She was forced to end her basketball career after she tore her anterior cruciate ligament. She missed an entire track and field season in 2000 while she recovered from her knee injury. Through a challenging rehabilitation period, Stephanie worked to strengthen her injured knee. She came back to finish fourth in the discus and third in the shot put in the NCAA Championships.

In the 2004 Olympic Trials, Stephanie fouled on her last five throws, but fortunately, she threw her best throw ever by more than nine feet on her first throw. It was enough for her to finish second and reach her goal of making the United States Olympic team. She finished 22nd in the Olympic Games. The trip to the Olympics motivated Stephanie to keep working hard. Many athletes train full time; however, Stephanie was one of the few athletes who worked a job while training.

Stephanie made dramatic improvements and qualified for the 2008 Olympic Games by placing third in the U.S. Olympic Trials. She improved her personal best that she had set more than four years earlier with a throw that was the third best American throw of all-time. Many experts did not predict Stephanie to be a medal contender despite the fact she had the second best throw in the world in the Olympic year. However, Stephanie had confidence that she had trained hard and was having her best year ever. In Beijing, she took the lead with her first throw and none of her competitors were able to beat her mark. Stephanie was the Olympic Champion! Her victory was one of the great surprises of the 2008 Olympics. It was the first gold medal for the United States in the women's discus since 1932.

In 2012 Stephanie set the American record with a throw of 222-3 in the discus and made her third Olympic team by winning the Olympic Trials. She made the Olympic final and placed eighth in the competition. With belief in herself and a strong work ethic, Stephanie made history at the Olympics by becoming an Olympic champion in an event the United States had not been traditionally strong.

Questions for Thought:

1. Stephanie stayed positive after injuries. How do you stay positive when you are hurt?

2. Stephanie was a big underdog when she won the gold medal. What is your thought when people think you cannot achieve something?

3. Stephanie's first Olympic Games motivated her to work harder. What successes have you had that have inspired you to work harder?

Zola Budd

The Barefoot Prodigy

At the age of 17, Zola Budd broke the world record for the women's 5000-meter run—running barefoot. However, her performance took place in South Africa, which was then excluded from international athletics competition because of its apartheid policy. The International Amateur Athletic Federation (I.A.A.F.) refused to ratify Zola's time as an official world record. Frustrated by the political turmoil in South Africa, she was able to gain British citizenship since her grandfather was British.

Zola qualified for the 1984 Olympic Games in Los Angeles and the media billed the women's 3000-meter race as a duel between Zola and American world champion Mary Decker. Decker set a fast pace from the gun with Zola in close pursuit, followed by Maria Puică of Romania and Wendy Smith-Sly of Great Britain. At the 1200-meter mark, the pace was slowing, so Zola took the lead to set the pace. At the 1700-meter point, Mary Decker, running half a stride behind Zola on the inside, contacted Zola's left foot, knocking her slightly off balance. Decker maintained her close position and again clipped Zola, striking the leader's calf with her right shoe. A third collision followed, and Decker stumbled and fell onto the infield. Her left hip injured, she was unable to resume the race.

Zola continued to lead for a while, but the pro-U.S. crowd rained down a chorus of boos, thinking she had fouled their favorite female distance runner, Decker. An I.A.A.F. jury later found that she was not responsible for the collision. However, reduced to tears, the young Zola faded, finishing seventh.

The next year, she was the world cross country champion, but never could beat Decker on the track. After sitting out a year with an injury, she began to compete again but was suspended from competition in a controversial decision about competing in her home country of South Africa. She retired from international competition for several years, but returned to represent South Africa in the 1992 Summer Olympics in Barcelona, competing in the 3000 meters.

Questions for Thought:

1. Zola was blamed for an accident that wasn't her fault. How would you react if you were in that situation?

2. Despite many obstacles, Zola continued her competitive career and remained a lifelong runner. Do you plan on exercising or running your entire life? Why?

3. Zola was looked upon as an athlete without a country. What would it be like to be without a team?

Tonya Buford-Bailey

Winning Attitude

At 12 years of age, Tonya Buford-Bailey met legendary track and field star Wilma Rudolph, who provided inspiration to the young track star. Tonya also received motivation from and dedicated her running to her sister, Crystal, who has muscular dystrophy.

Tonya won four state titles in the Ohio State Track and Field Championships (three in the 100-meter hurdles and one in the 300-meter hurdles). During her career at the University of Illinois, Tonya was a 10-time All-America selection and won a Big-Ten record 25 titles.

She started her Olympic career in 1992. She set the stage by winning the 400-meter hurdles at the NCAA Track and Field Championships and then finished second in the Olympic Trials. At the Olympic Games, she finished third in a semifinal heat but did not qualify for the final.

Her greatest race came in 1995 in the 400-meter hurdles final at the World Championships. Tonya and fellow American teammate Kim Batten were both running the race of their lives. They touched down off hurdle eight matching each other stride for stride over the last two hurdles. Kim won by a mere one-hundredth of a second over Tonya, with both athletes breaking the previous world record. Tonya's time of 52.62 remains one of the top 400-meter hurdle performances of all-time.

She made her second Olympic team in 1996, placing second in the Olympic Trials and earning a bronze medal, running 53.22 in a highly competitive 400-meter hurdle field.

Before the 2000 Olympic Games Tonya became a new mom. With limited training, she came back and made the 2000 U.S. Olympic team with a third place finish at the Olympic Trials in Sacramento and went on to place fourth in the first round heat of the Olympics but failed to advance further.

Using the same drive that propelled her to be a successful athlete, Tonya was very successful as the head women's track and field coach at the University of Illinois, before becoming a coach at the University of Texas.

Questions for Thought:

1. Tonya received motivation from her sister, who has muscular dystrophy. Do you receive motivation from someone who may not be as fortunate as you?

2. Tonya's meeting with Wilma Rudolph served as motivation. Do you have a role model who helps motivate you?

3. Tonya has become a very successful coach. Think about how your experiences will help shape your career?

Chi Cheng

Greatest Asian Sprinter of All Time

Chi Cheng was born and raised in Taiwan. As a 16-year-old, she competed in the 80-meter hurdles in the Rome 1960 Olympics. She was discovered by American coaches and came to the United States to study at Cal Poly Pomona in California.

In 1964, she participated in her second Olympics in Tokyo. Chi failed to win a medal after she finished 17th in the heptathlon, scoring 4449 points. She also ran in the 80-meter hurdles but failed to qualify for the final.

Chi was back for the 1968 Olympic Games in Mexico City, and despite having her training hampered by pulled muscles in both legs, she captured a bronze medal in the 80-meter hurdles. She also finished seventh in the 100 meters behind Wyomia Tyus, who won the race in a world record time of 11.0. Her Olympic bronze medal made her the first Asian woman in history to medal at the Olympics, and only Taiwan's second Olympian ever to win a medal. Chi was a hero in her homeland and her name was immortalized on national stamps.

In 1969, Chi won 66 of 67 competitions, and the following year, she was undefeated in 83 running, jumping, and hurdling events. She broke or tied three world records within the space of one week. In her career, she broke a total of seven world records over 100 yards, 100 meters, 200 meters, 220 yards, and 100-meter hurdles. Due to her perseverance, discipline, and talent, experts voted her as the "Best Athlete in the World" in 1971.

As the 1972 Olympics approached, she was expected to win at least one gold medal in Munich. But injuries struck and she had to undergo surgery. The injuries led to her retirement in 1973.

Chi was immensely popular in Taiwan and is considered the greatest Asian female sprinter of all-time. She was elected to the national senate in 1981.

Questions for Thought:

1. Chi excelled in a country not known for producing athletes. How can programs with little tradition rise to success?

2. Chi broke an incredible three world records in one week. How important is self-confidence? How would you rate your self-confidence?

3. After her running success, Chi used her talents to help her country. How can you contribute to society outside of the athletic arena?

Christine Clark

Ordinary Person with Extraordinary Desire

Christine Clark was a 37-year-old mom with two children— a 6 and 9-year-old. As a pathologist, she worked long hours. She lived in Anchorage, Alaska, an environment that only has an outdoor running season of five months. Training was extremely challenging so the odds were not good that Christine could make the U.S. Olympic team in the marathon, but she had been inspired more than 16 years earlier by watching Joan Benoit win the first Olympic women's marathon in 1984.

While most competitive marathoners logged 100 or 120 miles a week, Christine put in just 50 to 70 miles, most of them on a treadmill. She trained with one session of weight training a week and added some supplemental cross country skiing.

Christine ran in college at Montana State and was only moderately successful on the track, but starred academically, focusing on a biomedical science degree and obtaining a 3.99 grade point average. She continued to run through medical school and two pregnancies, but didn't race for several years while she completed her residency and started a family.

When she took up competitive running again, she qualified for the 1996 U.S. Olympic Marathon Trials and placed 76th in a time of 2:51:07. She continued to train on her treadmill in Alaska, often with the heat turned up high in the room. She again qualified for the U.S Olympic Marathon Trials in 2000, but faced a challenging field, which included several U.S. Olympians (including her hero, Joan Benoit) whom had run several minutes faster than Christine. Her goal was to finish in the top 20, which would have been quite an improvement from her previous Olympic Trials race.

The day of the 2000 Olympic Trials Marathon in Columbia, South Carolina, the temperatures soared to 84 degrees. The heat slowed the favorites, but didn't seem to have an effect on Christine, whose heat training had acclimated her for the conditions. She took the lead at mile 20 and crossed the finish line in a winning time of 2:33:31 to shock the field. Despite the heat, she had run a personal record by more than seven minutes! Representing the U.S. at the 2000 Olympic Games, Christine lowered her personal record even further with a 2:31:35 to finish 19th.

Christine Clark's victory at the 2000 Olympic Marathon Trials was one of the greatest upsets in U.S. Olympic Trials history. A late bloomer, Christine demonstrated that an ordinary person with extraordinary desire could fulfill dreams.

Questions for Thought:

1. What does the phrase, "ordinary person with extraordinary desire" mean to you?

2. Christine focused her attention on quality training. What does your quality training look like?

3. Christine adapted her training to meet her needs. How have you adapted to meet the situations you have faced?

Joetta Clark Diggs

A Family Affair

Joetta Clark Diggs is from an active and successful family. Her father, Joe Clark, was the high school principal portrayed in the movie, "Lean on Me." Her sister, Hazel Clark, and sister-in-law, Jearl Miles-Clark, were successful track stars, and her brother, Joe Clark, Jr., coached all three women.

Joetta was a star at Columbia High School in Maplewood, New Jersey. She developed a combination of speed and stamina that made her successful in the 800 meters. She was a state champion, a U.S. junior champion, and ran in the 1980 Olympic Trials as a high schooler, finishing in seventh place. She ran 2:04.5 for 800 meters, a national record that stood for 28 years.

Joetta was a nine-time NCAA champion at the University of Tennessee. She captured 12 U.S national titles, but her greatest claim to fame was making four Olympic teams in 1988, 1992, 1996, and 2000. Her highest finish was seventh in 1992. Her personal best time at 800 meters was 1:57.84.

At the 2000 Olympic Trials, the three Clarks (Joetta, her sister Hazel, and sister in-law Jearl) swept the 800-meter final, with Joetta, at age 37, finishing third to make her fourth Olympic team.

Joetta Clark made four Olympic teams and competed in six Olympic Trials over a span of 24 years. She has displayed more consistency and longevity than any other American middle distance runner. Her commitment to the sport has been a shining example of striving for good health and exhibiting a positive work ethic.

Questions for Thought:

1. Joetta Clark competed in six Olympic Trials. What factors keep a person going for that long?

2. Joetta took great pride in her work ethic. How would you rate your work ethic on a scale of 1-10?

3. What mental factors go into being consistent?

Alice Coachman

African-American Pioneer

Alice Coachman became the first black woman of any nationality to win a gold medal at the Olympics with her victory in the high jump at the 1948 Summer Games in London. Alice was born as the middle child to a family of 10 children in rural Georgia. Because her parents were poor, Alice had to pick cotton to help her family meet expenses while she was in elementary school. She liked to run, but her father would whip her when he caught her running because, "women weren't supposed to be running like that." But secretly, Alice continued to practice. Unable to afford shoes, she ran barefoot on the dirt roads near her house, practicing jumps over a crossbar made of rags tied together. Eventually, her parents, although still reluctant, allowed her to compete in track and field to improve her raw talent. She broke high school and then collegiate records by the time she was 16 years old.

Alice's biggest goal was to compete in the Olympic Games in 1940. But World War II forced the cancellation of the 1940 and 1944 Olympic Games. Alice became the U.S. national high jump champion and the first African American women selected for a U.S. Olympic team. On August 7, 1948, at age 25, Alice made history by becoming the first woman of African descent to win an Olympic gold medal. The high jump competition came down to D.J. Tyler of England and Alice, with both jumping an Olympic record 5-6¼; however, Alice won with the least number of misses.

Alice became the first African American woman to endorse an international product when the Coca-Cola Company featured her prominently on billboards along America's highways. Alice Coachman's Olympic gold medal paved the way for generations of African American athletes to achieve great success.

Questions for Thought:

1. Alice ran barefoot and practiced with a cross bar made of rags. How are some ways you have improvised to get the job done?

2. Do you feel it is a privilege or a right to participate in sports?

3. Women were not supposed to be running during Alice's era. What would you do if the right to participate in athletics was taken away from you?

Lilian Copeland

Standing Firm

Lillian Copeland was born in New York in 1904 to Polish Jewish immigrants. Her father died during her youth and the family moved to Los Angeles after her mother remarried. Lillian attended the University of Southern California and excelled in track and field, tennis, and basketball. She became the first woman from USC to compete in the Olympics.

The Amsterdam Olympics in 1928 was the first Olympics to include women's track and field. However, it did not include Lillian's favorite and best event, the shot put, in which she was a four-time national champion. Undeterred, Lillian entered and won the silver medal in the discus, throwing 121-8. Amazingly quick for a weight thrower, she was a member of a 4x110-yard relay team that set a national record in 1928.

At the 1932 Olympics in Los Angeles, before a home crowd, she improved from the previous Olympics and won the gold medal in the discus, throwing a world record toss of 133-2.

She set a remarkable six world records each in the shot put, discus, and javelin from 1925 to 1932. She did not get an opportunity to throw the shot put in the Olympic Games, because it wasn't until 1948 that the women's shot put would be contested in the Olympic Games. The women's javelin was contested beginning in 1932.

Despite being one of the top throwers in the world, at the peak of her career, she boycotted the 1936 Olympics in Berlin to protest the Nazi government's refusal to allow Jewish athletes on the German Olympic squad. Lillian Copeland was willing to sacrifice Olympic glory to take a firm stand for what she believed in.

Questions for Thought:

1. Lillian's best events were not on the Olympic program and she was denied an opportunity. How can you make the most of the opportunities you are given?

2. How do you react when you do not get opportunities you believe you deserve?

3. Lillian sacrificed glory for her beliefs. Would you be willing to make sacrifices to stand up for what you believe in?

Betty Cuthbert

Golden Girl

The 1956 Olympic Games were held in Melbourne, Australia. Betty Cuthbert grew up with her twin sister in a suburb of Sydney. At age 18, she spent most of her savings to buy tickets to attend the Olympics. However, she didn't need the tickets, because surprisingly, she was chosen to represent Australia in the Olympic Games. Although she was not even rated in the top 15 in the world in her events at the beginning of the year, she would make history. In nine days she won the 100 meters, 200 meters, and anchored the Australian 4x100-meter relay team to a gold medal. Her three golds made her the first Australian to ever win three gold medals in a single Olympic Games and she became the "Golden Girl" of Australia.

Betty was in peak form for the 1960 Olympics in Rome, but a torn leg muscle forced her to withdraw from the 100-meter competition and she wasn't able to start the 200 meters. She felt she had accomplished her athletic goals and decided to retire.

However, she did not remain retired, coming back for the 1964 Olympics in Tokyo. It was tough coming back and trying to work herself into top racing shape. The women she used to beat were now beating her, so Betty made the decision to move up to the 400 meters and won her fourth Olympic gold medal.

Five years later, she would be diagnosed with multiple sclerosis and be confined to a wheelchair. She has used the same courage and effort that won her gold on the track to devote her life to raising research funds for multiple sclerosis.

Questions for Thought:

1. Betty felt like she had more to accomplish, so she came out of retirement. Do you feel like you have more to accomplish?

2. Life didn't treat Betty fair when she was diagnosed with multiple sclerosis. Are you guaranteed that life will treat you fair?

3. If it doesn't treat you fair, what will your reaction be?

Mary Decker Slaney

Consistent Persistence

Mary Decker Slaney is the only athlete to hold every American record from 800 meters to 10,000 meters. She continues to own the U.S. women's records in the 1500 (3:57.12), mile (4:16.71) and 3000 (8:25.83). She was the first woman to win the prestigious Jesse Owens track and field award, given to the best track and field athlete in the United States.

Mary began her running career at age 11. Her extreme dedication to training and racing took her to the top of the running world, but she also paid an injury-laden price throughout her career. Only fourteen-years-old at the time, Mary was too young to compete in the 1972 Olympics; however, she ended the year ranked first in the U.S. and fourth in the world in the 800 meters. She ran the indoor mile in 4:40.1 to set her first world record.

After missing the 1976 Olympics with an injury, Mary was forced to miss another Olympics when the U.S. boycotted the 1980 Olympic Games in Moscow. Mary continued to dominate women's distance running in the early 1980's. Her greatest international achievement came at the 1983 World Championships in Helsinki, where she won the 1500 and 3000 meters, a feat that would become known as the "Decker Double" and helped earn her the title of Sports Illustrated's Sportsperson of the Year for 1983.

In 1984, Mary came into the Olympic Games in Los Angeles as the heavy favorite in the 3000 meters. Partway through the race, Mary and Zola Budd of Great Britain tangled feet, with Mary going down hard and unable to continue.

After the heart-breaking run and fall in the 1984 Olympics, Mary endured a series of painful injuries and remarkable recoveries (20 operations), as well as exercise-induced asthma. She carried the American flag at the opening ceremonies at the 1988 Olympics but failed to medal and did not qualify for the 1992 Olympic Games. Mary never gave up on her dreams and continued to be successful qualifying for the 5000 meters at the 1996 Olympics in Atlanta at age 37, but failed to make the final.

Mary Decker Slaney set 36 American and 17 world records and competed in four Olympic Games. She was unable to win an Olympic medal, but she is still considered America's greatest mid-distance runner.

Questions for Thought:

1. What will Mary best be remembered for?

2. Why did Mary continue to pursue her dream of an Olympic medal despite numerous injuries?

3. How would you respond if you were faced with an injury?

Gail Devers

Recovering to Achieve

Gail Devers was a shining young talent in the 100 meters and 100-meter hurdles. Her training program was going well for the 1988 Olympic Games, when she started suffering from headaches and vision loss. She was able to qualify for the U.S.A Olympic team in the 100-meter hurdles but was eliminated in the semifinals. After the Olympics, Gail's health continued to decline further.

Doctor after doctor failed to diagnose her illness, as she suffered debilitating fatigue, losing nearly all her hair. After more than two years, Gail was finally diagnosed with a thyroid disease. She was treated with radioactive iodine to disable her thyroid. Fearing she would be banned from competition for using banned substances, Gail refused the drugs that were intended to diminish side effects from the radiation therapy required to treat her enlarged thyroid. Gail developed excruciatingly painful lesions on her feet and sores and scales all over her body and face. Her weight dropped from 125 to only 87 pounds, as she grew weaker and weaker. Gail was so distraught over her appearance that she covered all the mirrors in her Los Angeles home.

Her feet swelled so severely that the 5-3 runner could squeeze only into a size-12 men's sneaker and eventually she couldn't walk at all. Family members had to carry her to the bathroom. Her feet grew so swollen and infected that medical authorities believed they might require amputation, a diagnosis Gail fought against. Eventually, recovery came as Gail began a lifelong program of thyroid hormone replacement therapy.

Remarkably, Gail began to run again. At first, she rode a stationary bike at trackside, then she walked, then jogged, and eventually began to sprint and jump. The amazing Gail not only ran, she qualified for the 1992 Olympics Games in both the 100-meter hurdles and 100-meter dash. The Barcelona Olympics 100-meter dash was one of the closest in history, with five women within six one-hundredths of a second. After a long wait for results, the photo finish showed Gail as the winner. In the finals of the hurdles, she was leading into the final hurdle when disaster struck as she hit the last hurdle, stumbling across in fifth place.

In 1996, Gail again qualified for both the 100 meters and 100-meter hurdles Olympic final in Atlanta. In the 100-meter final, Merlene Ottey of Jamaica and Gail finished in the same time, with neither knowing who had won. Both were awarded the same time, but Gail was judged to have finished first. In the final of her favorite event, the 100-meter hurdles, she finished fourth.

Questions for Thought:

1. Gail Devers, recognized for competing with her long nails and powerful speed, left a legacy of a lesson about recovery and achievement. What did you learn from the story?

2. How do your problems compare to what Gail went through?

3. How do you stay determined when facing adversity?

Tirunesh Dibaba

Baby Faced Destroyer

Tirunesh Dibaba was born in the village of Bekoji, Ethiopia, and began her athletic career at age 14. She was so frail in physique that it was thought she would not be able to meet the physical demands of running. But Tirunesh persevered, and in 2003 at the age of 18, she became the youngest athlete ever to win a gold medal at the World Championships when she won the 5000 meters.

In the 2004 Olympics in Athens she finished third in the 5000 meters, a disappointment to her, but she was only 19 years of age.

At the World Championships in 2005, she became the first woman to win the 5000 and 10,000-meter double in the World Championships. Tirunesh's incredible sprint finish, which earned her the nickname Baby Faced Destroyer, is a trademark of her running style. She ran 58.33 on the last lap in the 10,000 meters at the World Championships. The following World Championships she endured abdominal pain throughout the 10,000-meter race and was tripped and fell midway. Undeterred, Tirunesh battled back and won.

2008 was a memorable year for Tirunesh. She set a 5000-meter world record of 14:11.16 and won both the 5000 and 10,000 meters in the Beijing Olympics, becoming the first woman ever to win both at the same Olympics.

Tirunesh returned to her third Olympics in 2012 and dominated the field over the last 600 meters to defend her 10,000-meter title. She also finished third in the 5000 meters to win her fifth Olympic medal.

As good as Tirnuesh was on the track, she was just as good in cross country, winning five World Cross Country Championships. She has established herself as one of history's greatest female distance runners.

Questions for Thought:

1. Tirunesh appears small and fragile, yet she is a tremendous competitor. How important is heart in athletic performance?

2. Tirunesh has a big kick. What physical and mental components go in to a big kick?

3. Tirunesh made history by winning a distance double in the Olympics. What do you believe is the key to pulling off a successful double?

Mildred "Babe" Didrickson Zaharias

Multi-Sport Star

Mildred "Babe" Didrickson Zaharias was born in Texas to parents from Norway. After a hurricane that killed 275 people destroyed their home, they moved to Beaumont, Texas. Times were tough for the large Didrickson family and Mildred worked at many part-time jobs. Her father believed in physical conditioning and built a weight set out of a broomstick and flat irons for the kids to work out with. Babe got her nickname after hitting five home runs in one baseball game (Babe Ruth was a star baseball player at the time), a nickname that remained with her for the rest of her life. Babe was also an outstanding basketball player and earned A.A.U. All-American honors.

The 1932 A.A.U. Championships in Evanston, Illinois, served as the Olympic track and field team qualifier and Babe score 30 points by herself, more than any other team. The second place team consisting of 22 athletes had 22 points. Within a three hour period, she competed in eight of the 10 events, winning six of them, and set world records in the javelin, 80-meter hurdles, high jump, and baseball throw.

Although she qualified for the 1932 Olympics in several events, women were only allowed to compete in three events. Babe threw the javelin 143-4 to set an Olympic and world record. She won the 80-meter hurdles in world record time and set her sights on the high jump. She cleared 5-5¼, which would have been a world record but officials ruled she had dived over the bar instead of jumping feet first and had to settle for second place. While Babe had jumped in the same manner throughout the competition, nothing was said to her about her style being illegal until after her final jump. The high jump rule was later changed. She remains the only athlete in Olympic history with individual medals in running, jumping, and throwing.

She turned to golf after the Olympics and became a dominant women's golfer, often called the greatest women's golfer of all time.

Babe Didrickson was a natural at sports, but it was her willingness to practice endlessly and her continual hard work that allowed her climb to the top and stay on top. Her competitive spirit and will to win made her a champion.

Questions for Thought:

1. Babe loved doing multiple events and was willing to try anything. Do you have the courage to step out and try new things?

2. Babe had natural talent, but worked hard to get better. Are you developing your talents to the fullest?

3. What could you do to further develop your talents?

Stacy Dragila

Raising The Bar For Females

Stacy Dragila's first love was actually gymnastics; however, when she developed childhood asthma, she had to give up the sport. Looking for a replacement, she began focusing on rodeo. She also played volleyball and was a sprinter, hurdler, and long jumper in track. Stacey attended Yuba Community College and was coached by John Orognen, who noticed her tremendous versatility, and encouraged her to try the heptathlon. Stacy and coach Orognen developed a close coach-athlete relationship. Unfortunately, Orognen developed lung cancer and died before Stacy finished her sophomore year. On his deathbed he advised her to pursue her dreams.

Stacy continued her education at Idaho State University as a heptathlete. Her heptathlon scores were respectable, but she was not a national-caliber contender. The women's pole vault was just taking off and female athletes were challenging the long-held belief that women lacked the upper body strength and mental toughness to excel in pole vaulting. Coach Nielsen realized that Stacy might be perfect for pole vaulting, being tall and muscular and with a background as a sprinter and a love of gymnastics. Initially she was not very good, but gradually she improved. Stacy started by clearing 10 feet, then 11feet, and in two years' time, she had improved to over 12 feet to become the second-best pole vaulter in the United States. After she graduated from college she stayed at Idaho State as an assistant coach and moonlighted as a waitress to make ends meet while she continued to train.

Stacy continued to improve, establishing a new world record of 14-7½. Stacy had her sights set on 15 feet when a stress fracture to her right foot required surgery. With women's vaulting becoming so popular, the International Olympic Committee had little choice but to announce its inclusion in the 2000 Summer Games in Sydney. The chance to win Olympic gold was a big source of motivation for Stacy. The night before the U.S. Olympic Trials Stacy experienced an anxiety attack. Stacy began to work on visualization exercises to help her relax and build back her confidence. Stacy secured a spot on the squad and set a new world record in the process, clearing 15-2¼.

Stacy arrived in Sydney as the favorite to win the first Olympic gold medal in women's pole vaulting. The fight for the gold came down to a three-way battle. When her competitors each cleared 14-9 and Stacy missed twice, the heat was on. In the past, that kind of pressure always did Stacy in, but she nailed her third attempt. She went on to clear 15-1 to win the first Olympic gold in the event.

Questions for Thought:

1. It took Stacy awhile to be successful in the pole vault. When you try something new, how do you "give it a chance" to see if you will succeed?

2. Early in her career, Stacy struggled with being positive and confident. When she practiced the mental game, her career took off. How much time do you put into mental training?

3. Stacy had an exciting opportunity to promote women's pole vaulting. What exciting opportunities lie ahead of you?

Deena Drossin Kastor

Making The Sacrifices

Deena Drossin Kastor's success was not an overnight achievement. She began with age group athletics and continued through high school, where she won three California state cross country titles and two state track titles. She also competed in the Foot Locker Cross Country Championships all four years of her prep career. At the University of Arkansas, she was a four-time SEC Conference champion and an eight-time All-American, but never a national champion. Her collegiate career was good, but not considered exceptional. The outstanding talent she displayed as a high school runner was never realized in college.

After graduation, Deena found herself with a burning desire to continue her training and dreamed of running in the Olympics. An assistant collegiate coach recommended she contact coach Joe Vigil, the outstanding distance coach of Adams State University, Colorado, and Olympic distance teams. At first, Vigil was reluctant to work with Deena and even tried to discourage her from moving to Alamosa. However, Deena was persistent and moved to Alamosa, taking a job as a dishwasher to make ends meet. Her persistence, hunger for high goals, and willingness to relocate to Alamosa, with an altitude of 7,543 feet, persuaded Vigil to coach her. Coach Vigil and Deena formed a successful team and developed mutual respect for one another.

Deena made her first Olympic team in 2004 by finishing second in the U.S. Olympic Trials Marathon. At the 2004 Olympics Games, Deena's brilliant and calculated strategy paid off. As the race unfolded on a challenging course and temperatures in the mid-80s with 50 percent humidity, Deena worked her way up through the field and executed a near-perfect race to earn an Olympic bronze medal in the women's marathon.

She was back at the 2008 Olympics with a goal of improving on her third place finish. At the 5-kilometer mark, she dropped to one knee, holding her right foot. Although she attempted to continue to run, she was forced to withdraw from the race due to a broken foot.

Through her hard work ethic and commitment to training, Deena developed into one of the greatest female runners in United States history.

Questions for Thought:

1. Deena's training included running more than 100 miles per week to finally reach her potential. How will you go about reaching your potential?

2. Deena was willing to relocate to be successful. What things are you willing to give up to reach your goals?

3. Deena's tactical strategy paid off for an Olympic medal. How do you develop your strategy when you go into a competition?

Allyson Felix

Strikes Gold

Photo by Spencer Allen

As a junior in high school, Allyson Felix won the 100 and 200 meters state titles with the top times in the nation for athletes under 20 years of age. In her senior year she repeated as the state champion, giving her five California state titles. She was ranked as the eighth best 200-meter runner in the world and set a United States record for athletes under age 20.

After graduating from high school, Allyson decided to turn professional and signed a contract with Adidas. Allyson was training for the 2004 Olympics when she was diagnosed with exercise-induced asthma. At only 18 years of age, Allyson made the 2004 U.S. Olympic team in the 200 meters and was the youngest person on the United States team. She won the 2004 Olympic Trials and finished second in the Olympic Games in Athens, running a personal best time and setting a world junior record for athletes under age 20.

She was one of the favorites to win the gold medal at the 2008 Olympic Games in Beijing, China. Allyson raced against Veronica Campbell-Brown of Jamaica, who was the defending Olympic champion. Although Allyson crossed the finish line with a season best time, it was not fast enough to beat Campbell, and Allyson settled for her second straight Olympic silver medal in the 200 meters. Allyson came back later and won her first Olympic gold medal running on the 4x400-meter relay team.

Still searching for the individual Olympic gold medal to complete her resume, Allyson competed in the 100 and 200 meters at the 2012 Olympic Trials. She won the 200 in a personal best and a meet record time of 21.69 and tied for third in a controversial 100-meter race with Jeneba Tarmoh. She received the 100-meter Olympic berth when Tarmoh pulled out of a run-off.

At the 2012 Olympics she competed in four events: the 100 meters, 200 meters, 4x100-meter relay, and the 4x400-meter relay. She placed fifth in the 100 meters, but finally struck individual gold in the 200 meters. She also added gold in the two relays and a world record in the 4x100-meter relay. Allyson is a shining star in the world of athletics and serves as a positive role model for female athletes. She stands strongly against drug use and works with children to promote the positive image of track and field.

Questions for Thought:

1. Allyson had been to two previous Olympics but failed to win an individual gold, finishing second twice. How do you feel when you repeatedly fall short of your goals?

2. Allyson won four medals in London, including two from relay events. How are you a team contributor?

3. Allyson is a great role model for young athletes. What characteristics do you have that would make you a great role model? How do you develop those characteristics?

Shalane Flanagan

Versatile Runner

*Photo by Pretty Sporty/
Cheryl Treworgy*

Shalane Flanagan grew up in Marblehead, Massachusetts, the daughter of two elite runners. Her mother once owned the American record at 5000 meters and the world record in the marathon and her father was a world-class marathoner. Growing up, Shalane participated in soccer and swimming as well as cross country and track. She was a three-time high school all-state cross country performer and won state championships in the mile and two mile.

At the University of North Carolina, she won two NCAA cross country titles and a NCAA Indoor 3000 meters title. She made her first Olympic team in the 5000 meters but did not advance from her heat at the 2004 Olympic Games.

After turning professional, Shalane suffered increased pain in her left foot. She visited numerous different doctors before one finally discovered that she was born with an extra bone in her foot. The bone was tearing a tendon so the bone was removed and the tendon repaired. The surgery took her out of the 2006 season, but she came back the following year more determined than ever.

Shalane set the U.S. indoor 3000-meter record (8:33.25) and the outdoor 5000-meter record (14:44.90) in 2007. The following year she ran the 10,000 meters for the first time and set an American record of 30:50.32. At the 2008 Olympic Trials, Shalane ran the 5000 and 10,000 meters, winning the 10,000 meters and placing third in the 5000 meters to make her second Olympic team. Competing at the highest level, Shalane had her finest hour in the 2008 Olympic Games in Beijing. She finished in third place in the 10,000, shattering her old American record (30:22.22) and winning the only distance medal for the U.S. in the Beijing Olympic Games. She became only the second American woman ever to win an Olympic medal in the 10,000 meters. She was also 10th in the 5000-meter race.

Shalane moved up to the marathon in 2010 debuting at the New York City marathon with a time of 2:28.49, the best finish by an American woman in that race in 20 years. Shalane decided to run the marathon at the 2012 Olympics and won the U.S. Olympic Trials marathon, setting a meet record of 2:25.38 to make her third Olympic team. In London, Shalane ran against one of the strongest marathon fields ever assembled and finished a highly respectable 10th place in only her third marathon.

Questions for Thought:

1. Shalane has been a versatile runner during her career. How do you go about being more versatile?

2. Shalane had the courage to move up in distance. How do you define courage?

3. Shalane grew up in a running environment. How do you create a successful environment for yourself and others?

Jane Frederick

First Great American Multi-Eventer

Jane Frederick attended track meets with her father as a child. The meets caught her interest and she joined a youth track and field club at age 11. At only 13 years of age she entered the national pentathlon championship even though the age limit was 14 and placed fifth. The early success encouraged her to start training seriously. Jane attended the University of Colorado, but at the time the school had no women's track program. Jane's college choice was based on receiving a quality education. A 3.5-GPA student in college, Jane spoke five languages and credited her academic pursuits as helping her in track.

At Colorado she started working out with coach Lyle Knudson. Just as she was starting to get serious about track she tore a hamstring. It was 14 months later before she entered a meet. In the meantime Jane decided to major in art and spent a year studying in Pisa, Italy. She met an Italian coach, Franco Radman, who put her on a weight-lifting program and convinced her that she could qualify for the 1972 Olympics as a pentathlete. Jane returned to Colorado and her focused training enabled her to win her first national pentathlon title at the 1972 Olympic Trials.

As Jane approached the 1972 Olympics she viewed herself as a dedicated athlete, and by most standards she was. However, what she discovered in Munich, where she placed 21st, changed her career. Jane said, "When I got to Munich I saw just how much I had been playing around. I saw that the pentathlon had to be the central focus of my life, not just an activity on the side. I had always known I could do better but now I saw how much more I had to do to achieve something significant. And I said to myself, 'Okay. That's what I want to do.'

Jane focused on her training for the following Olympic Games of 1976 in Montreal. She had high hopes, but failed to meet her expectation of medaling. She was sixth at the end of the first day and finished seventh. A hamstring injury kept her out of the 1980 Olympic Trials but she came back to set the first official world record in the women's heptathlon, scoring 6104 points in 1981. When she began the pentathlon at age 13 the events were the 100-meter hurdles, high jump, long jump, shot put and 200-meter dash. In 1977, the 800 meters replaced the 200. In 1981, the pentathlon was expanded to a heptathlon and the javelin and 200 meters were added. Considered one of the top U.S. women's combined-events athletes in history, Jane's 23-year career was remarkable as she set the standard for all future multi-event competitors by setting 22 American records in the multi-events.

Questions for Thought:

1. Jane placed a strong emphasis on her education and credited it with helping her in track. How does your academic work assist you athletically?

2. At her first Olympic Games Jane realized how hard she would have to work to succeed. How can you take your practice habits to the next level?

3. Jane competed for 23 years because she enjoyed the self-satisfaction with the sport. How motivating is self-satisfaction as a reward?

Cathy Freeman

Carrying The Hopes of a Nation

From an early age, Cathy Freeman realized that she not only loved to run, but that she was good at it. Cathy's family did not have a lot of money and like many Australian Aboriginals, suffered discrimination from white Australians. At a primary school competition, she had to watch as the white girls she had beaten received trophies, and she was not given a trophy.

As she continued to have success in track, she began to dream about being an Olympic champion and began to focus on training that would help her achieve her dream. At the 1990 Commonwealth Games in Auckland, New Zealand, Cathy won a gold medal as a member of the 4x100-meter relay team, becoming the first female Australian Aboriginal to win a gold medal at an international athletics event. By 1992, she had qualified for her first Olympic Games in Seoul, South Korea, becoming the first Australian Aboriginal to represent Australia at an Olympics, and she reached the second round in the 400 meters.

Cathy won gold in both the 200 meters and 400 meters in the 1994 Commonwealth Games and had become one of the world's best sprinters. She also competed as a member of Australia's 4x100-meter relay team, winning the silver medal and as a member of the 4x400-relay team that finished first but was later disqualified.

Cathy continued to progress during the 1996 season, setting many personal bests and Australian records. On the world stage, she competed in the 1996 Olympic Games in Atlanta. In an exciting 400-meter race, Cathy led for much of the distance, until Marie-José Pérec of France closed the gap and took the lead in the last 80 meters. It took an Olympic record by Pérec to beat Cathy, who took the silver medal in a new Australian record of 48.63.

Cathy had developed into the favorite to win the 400-meter Olympic title in 2000 in Sydney, Australia. The pressure of being the favorite was enormous, as she not only carried the Australian hopes; she carried the hopes of all Aborigines. To add to the pressure, Cathy was chosen to carry the Australian flag in the opening ceremonies. Despite the enormous pressure, Cathy was able to focus on the task, and dominated the Olympic field on her way to the title. After the race, Cathy took a victory lap, carrying both the Aboriginal and Australian flags. She also finished sixth in the 200 meters and fifth in the 4x400-meter relay.

Questions for Thought:

1. Cathy Freeman had enormous pressure to win and she came through. How do you handle pressure?

2. Cathy faced discrimination growing up and overcame it to help unite a nation. If you have been discriminated against, what did it feel like?

3. How do you maintain focus when you have many distractions surrounding you?

Kara Goucher

Patience is a Virtue

Kara Goucher was born in Queens, New York. When she was only 4 years old, her father was killed by a drunk driver. Kara attended college and starred at the University of Colorado, becoming the NCAA Indoor Champion in the 3000 meters and NCAA Outdoor Champion in the 5000 meters, as well as the NCAA Cross Country Champion.

The road to success is not always a straight path, and Kara's career hit a sharp detour as she was slowed down by injuries such as numerous stress fractures, knee injuries, and compartment syndrome for several years. She became frustrated and almost gave up running. However, in 2005, Kara and her husband Adam, also a star runner and NCAA champion at Colorado, moved to Portland, Oregon to train and to be coached by the famous marathon runner, Alberto Salazar. This was part of the Nike Oregon Project, a project designed to improve standards in American distance running. With support from Nike, they made training a full-time job. With two runs a day, hours of drills, stretching, running in the pool, and weightlifting, she developed into one of the top female distance runners in the United States.

Photo by Pretty Sporty/ Cheryl Treworgy

Her commitment and dedication paid off in 2007 at the IAAF World Championships in Osaka, Japan, where she won the bronze medal in the women's 10,000-meter event, and her time made her the second fastest American woman of all-time. Kara competed in the Beijing 2008 Summer Olympics 10,000-meter final, where she placed 10th with a personal best time of 30:55.16, and the 5000-meter, where she placed ninth with a time of 15:49.39. Her success story continued as she made her marathon debut at the New York City Marathon in 2008, finishing in third place.

Kara gave birth to a son, Colt, in 2010, and in 2011 she switched coaches to train with Jerry Schumacher. Kara qualified for the 2012 Olympics Marathon, but in London she finished a disappointing 11th place in 2:26:07.

Kara Goucher's career has been full of frustration with numerous leg injuries; however, she has remained patient and positive. Through her persistence, she has been able to reach her potential.

Questions for Thought:

1. What makes Kara Goucher one of the top runners in the United States?

2. Kara's patience paid off. How can your patience pay off?

3. Do you expect success overnight, or are you patient and improve one day at a time?

Ana Guevera

No Limits

Ana Guevara's dream was to make the Mexican national basketball team. When she failed to make the basketball team, she was heartbroken and turned to track and field. She found her talent was in the 400-meter dash, but she struggled financially to be able to compete.

As a 23-year-old, she qualified for the 2000 Sydney Olympics in the 400-meter final, and finished in fifth place with a time of 49.96.

Ana often celebrated her victories by carrying the Mexican flag high above her head, proud of her Mexican heritage. She was selected as the flag bearer for the Mexican Olympic team in 2004, when she represented her country in the 400 meters. After winning her heat in the first round and the corresponding semifinal, she won the silver medal in the final.

Her career included 24 consecutive international victories, a Mexican national record, a world leading time, and a No. 1 ranking in the world. Her personal best in the 400 meters was 48.89, which is one of the fastest times in history.

But Ana Guevara's legacy is about much more than breaking records. It's about breaking stereotypes. Only one percent of Mexican women older than age 20 run. Her goal is to encourage more Mexican women to become active and to strive to achieve challenging goals. Ana Guevara's experiences in track and field stand as a shining example for the Mexican woman of the 21st century, showing that there are no limits.

Questions for Thought:

1. Ana turned heartbreak into success. Do you have experiences where you went from heartbreak to success?

2. Ana has led by example. Why is it important for athletes to lead by example?

3. What does the phrase "no limits" mean to you?

Dawn Harper

The Improbable Champion

Photo by Spencer Allen

Dawn Harper grew up in East Saint Louis, Illinois. With talent and a love for running, Dawn started as a sprinter in track and field competitions. In the seventh grade she started running hurdles. Her career in high school yielded six Illinois state championships and she went on to the University of California at Los Angeles (UCLA) to compete, becoming a seven-time All-American.

Dawn turned professional and was off to a great start when a minor ache turned into a major problem. Dawn had to have knee surgery and could not train for two months. She refused to give up her dream and kept her spirit up, bouncing back more determined than ever. She competed in the 2008 Olympic Trials in Eugene, Oregon and placed third by less than one one-hundredth of a second, barely qualifying for the Olympic team in the 100-meter hurdles.

At the 2008 Beijing Olympic Games, the U.S. team was expected to sweep the 100-meter hurdles. Lolo Jones was the favorite with Dawn considered the underdog. She had lost her shoe contract and even had to borrow spikes from a friend before the race. Jones got out fast and appeared to be headed to victory; however, at the last hurdle, Jones clipped a hurdle and began stumbling. Dawn came off the final hurdle and leaned for the finish line, but her legs went out from underneath her, so she hit the track and was able to tuck and roll past the finish line. Dawn Harper had shocked the world. Fighting back from an injury, a virtual unknown had hurdled her way to become the Olympic champion!

Dawn suffered another career-threatening injury in 2010 and was told she may never hurdle again. After a lengthy rehabilitation from a second knee surgery, she returned to hurdling in 2011 determined to prove her Olympic title was not a fluke. She started her journey back by winning the 2012 Trials.

The 2012 Olympic Games in London featured the deepest 100-meter hurdle final in history. The race lived up to its billing, with Dawn running a personal best of 12.37 to capture the silver medal, just missing the gold by two-one hundredths of a second from Australian Sally Pearson. Dawn has a strong passion for being a role model and working with kids, encouraging them with hope that anyone can reach their dreams.

Questions for Thought:

1. Dawn Harper was the underdog but came out on top. What do you focus on if you are the underdog?

2. Dawn never gave up on her dreams and stayed positive. How hard is it to be positive when things go against you?

3. Dawn is a strong role model for children. In what ways are you a positive role model?

Queen Harrison

Running Like Royalty

With a name like Queen, you are expected to be great in what you do. Queen Harrison has lived up to her name. Her father has 23 children, nine with her mother. When Queen was growing up, her father, a former paratrooper who served in Vietnam, awakened her and her siblings each morning for a regimen of running, jumping jacks, sit-ups, and push-ups before school to teach his kids to be disciplined.

The exercises paid off in high school, as Harrison won Virginia State Championships in the long jump and the triple jump. As a freshman at Virginia Tech, she set a school record of 55.81 in the 400-meter hurdles, while placing third at the 2007 NCAA Championships. As a sophomore, Queen was one of the favorites to win the NCAA Championships in both the 100-meter hurdles and the 400-meter hurdles. But disaster struck when she was running on Virginia Tech's 4x100-meter relay team in a preliminary round. Queen strained her hamstring and had to withdraw from the meet. The 2008 Olympic Trials were only a few weeks away and her dream of competing in the Olympics seemed to be over. However, intense rehabilitation got her ready to run in the Olympic Trials.

Queen also had to overcome the fact that her biggest supporter, her dad, had been sentenced to prison and now was unable to see her run. Queen advanced through the early rounds of the 400-meter hurdles in the Olympic Trials to qualify for the final, but drew lane eight. Lane eight is considered one of the worst lanes because on the outside you cannot see your competitors. Queen was in contention throughout the race. As she came down the homestretch, Queen was running in fourth place over the ninth hurdle. With one hurdle to go, she needed to improve her position if she was to achieve her Olympic dream. Suddenly, Miriam Barnes, running in lane seven, fell directly into Queen's lane and she had to hurdle the fallen Barnes to move into third. Finishing strong as she drove to the finish line, she finished second behind only Tiffany Ross-Williams. The 19-year-old Harrison became one of the youngest members of the United States team for the Beijing Games.

At the 2008 Summer Olympics, Queen was eliminated after finishing seventh in the 400-meter hurdles semifinals, finishing with a time of 55.88. In 2010, Queen became the first female in NCAA history to win both the 100 and 400-meter hurdles national titles at the same NCAA Championships and was awarded the Bowerman Award as the most outstanding female athlete in collegiate track and field.

Questions for Thought:

1. Queen Harrison attributed making the Olympic team to her mental power and confidence. How mentally tough do you consider yourself to be?

2. Queen had to jump 11 hurdles, one being a human, to make the U.S. team. What hurdles may unexpectedly appear in your way? How will you handle them?

3. During the course of an event, something unpredictable may arise. How can you prepare for the unpredictable?

Joanna Hayes

Passion to Return

Joanna Hayes was born in Williamsport, Pennsylvania, and moved to California at 4 years of age. At John W. North High School, Joanna was a state champion in the 100 and 300-meter hurdles, as well as a national and Pan Am Champion, and was named the National High School Athlete of the Year in 1995.

Joanna's early career was beset by injury. She suffered a hyper-extended knee in 1997 during the NCAA Outdoor Championships. Although the injury kept her from competing in the 100-meter hurdles, Joanna ran the anchor leg on UCLA's 4x100-meter relay team that placed sixth (44.76), and she placed seventh (57.92) in the final of the 400-meter hurdles. Despite a series of injuries, Joanna eventually became a national champion at UCLA.

Photo by Pretty Sporty/
Cheryl Treworgy

Joanna took some time off to work at the Jackie Joyner-Kersee Youth Center East St. Louis, Illinois, but returned to Los Angeles to train full time in preparation for the 2000 Olympic Games. She narrowly missed a spot on the 2000 U.S. Olympic Team, placing fourth in the 400-meter hurdles and fifth in the 100-meter hurdles.

After her career at UCLA, Joanna turned professional and won the gold medal in the 100-meter hurdles at the 2004 Olympics in Athens in an Olympic record time of 12.37, becoming only the second American in history to win the title.

In the 2008 Olympic Trials, she tore a patellar tendon in her knee, limping off the track, intending on never hurdling again. However, her competitive instincts resurfaced, and at age 35 and as the mother of a young daughter, Joanna made her return. Despite a limited racing schedule in 2012, she trained to earn a spot on the London team. Joanna raced through the first round, but the field of U.S. hurdlers was the best in the world and she could advance no further in the trials and failed to make the Olympic team.

Just as her father and mother worked to help homeless people, Joanna formed a foundation, the Joanna Hayes Foundation, to help broaden the horizons of children living in challenging situations to prepare them for new, realistic, and hopeful futures.

Questions for Thought:

1. Joanna's competitive instincts encouraged her to return to compete in her fourth Olympic Trials. On a scale of 1-10, what kind of a competitor are you?

2. Joanna gives back to her community. What are you willing to give back to those who have helped you?

3. What are some practical ways you can assist those who are in need of help?

Kelly Holmes

Handling the Pressure

Kelly Holmes grew up in England and started training for athletics at the age of 12. The British middle distance star, Steve Ovett, and his success at the 1980 Olympics inspired her. After a successful youth career at 1500 meters, Kelly left school and gave up running. She eventually joined the army.

Kelly watched the 1992 Summer Olympics on television and saw athletes she had beaten before competing in the Olympic Games. Motivated, she returned to training, balancing her duties for the army with her training.

Her accomplishments over the next few years would be marred by injuries and depression. She suffered allergies, anemia, and back problems. She had the Epstein Barr virus and chronic fatigue. She faced ovarian surgery, hamstring pulls, and stress fractures. She tore an Achilles tendon and ruptured a calf muscle, as well as damaging her femoral nerve.

When she was healthy, she had enough success to encourage her to persevere. She won a bronze medal in the 2000 Olympics. As she was training for the 2004 Olympics, Kelly suffered more injuries and became depressed. Being a professional athlete can be extremely difficult, placing athletes under tremendous amounts of stress. Kelly began cutting herself, making one cut for every day she had been injured. She considered suicide, but fortunately sought help and was diagnosed with clinical depression.

With her depression under control, she re-focused on her 20-year ambition of Olympic gold, even though she knew she would, at the age of 34, have to become the oldest Olympic champion in her events in history to succeed.

She competed in both the 800 and 1500 meters in the 2004 Olympics. The 800 meters was up first and Kelly ran a smart race, ignoring the fast start by a number of runners and moved to the lead on the final curve to win the gold medal. She used the same strategy in the 1500 meters to win gold again, running 3:57.90 to set a new British record. Her double gold wins earned her the honor of carrying the British flag at the closing ceremony.

Questions for Thought:

1. Kelly Holmes felt the pressure. How do you respond to what you perceive to be overwhelming situations?

2. Kelly realized she needed help and sought it. Are you willing to ask for help if you need it?

3. Despite her injuries, Kelly persevered over a long time period. How frustrating is it to have setbacks? How can you deal with setbacks?

Lynn Jennings

Drive Ambition

When Lynn Jennings attended Bromfield High School in Massachusetts, she ran on the boys' cross country team because there was no girls' team. Her first year as a freshman, she was last in every race and at all of the practices. That humbling experience helped develop her competitive will and mental discipline, skills that would serve her well in her successful career. Her competitive nature propelled her to improve to become one of the best high school runners in the country.

She went to Princeton University and earned All-American honors and set several school records and had a mixture of success and setbacks. The setbacks only seemed to fire up her determination. As she turned professional, her discipline in training and racing became legendary in track and field circles.

She ran in the 1984 Olympic Trials but fared so poorly she considered giving up running. But in 1984, Lynn witnessed American Joan Benoit win the first women's Olympic Marathon. The victory was especially inspiring for Lynn because not only had she raced Benoit before, she had beaten her.

Lynn thrived in cross country, training through brutal winters in New Hampshire. She won three straight world cross country titles from 1990 to 1992. She made the U.S. Olympic team in 1988 and competed in the Olympic 10,000 meters, finishing in sixth place.

She made her second Olympic team in 1992 and earned a bronze medal in the 10,000 meters at the 1992 Olympics, setting an American record in 31:19.89. She made her third Olympic team in 1996 and ran the 5000 meters in the 1996 Atlanta Olympics.

As a world cross country champion, Olympian, and American record holder, Lynn Jennings ran all the way to the history books as one of the greatest distance runners the U.S. has ever produced.

Questions for Thought:

1. Lynn finished last in every practice and race her first year of running cross country. Would you have continued in that situation?

2. What toughness did Lynn develop from having to compete on the boys' team?

3. Lynn's discipline is legendary. How would you rate your discipline? What steps could you take to be more disciplined?

Jackie Joyner-Kersee

World's Greatest Female Athlete

Jackie Joyner-Kersee grew up in a violent neighborhood, witnessing murder and violence on the streets; however, her parents created an environment of love and a work ethic to achieve goals. Although drugs and alcohol surrounded her in her neighborhood, Jackie stayed away from that path and excelled in the classroom as an honor student. She began to show her promise as an athlete by long jumping over 17 feet when she was only 12 years old.

Jackie attended college at UCLA, but as an 18-year-old freshman, Jackie had to return home due to the tragic death of her 37-year-old mother, Mary, from a rare form of meningitis. Mary had been Jackie's inspiration and Jackie's grief threatened to derail her academic and athletic career. Jackie worked hard to perfect her skills and won the NCAA heptathlon two years in a row as well as the 1982 U.S. Championship. As Jackie prepared to compete in the 1983 World Championships in Helsinki, Finland, she pulled a hamstring and was forced to withdraw. She was also diagnosed with an asthmatic condition requiring constant medication, another challenge she would struggle with but consistently overcome.

In the 1984 Olympic Games in Los Angeles, California, Jackie had the lead in the heptathlon going into the final event, the 800 meters. However, her hamstring injury slowed her down and she ran less than a second too slow to win, with Glynis Nunn of Australia winning the gold by a margin of a mere five points. Jackie's career continued to soar as she tied the world record of 24-5½ inches in the long jump.

At the 1988 Olympic Games, Jackie won gold medals in both the heptathlon and long jump. She also won a bronze medal in the long jump at the 1992 Olympic Games. The 1996 Olympic Games were held in Atlanta, Georgia, and Jackie had an opportunity to compete for gold in the heptathlon. Again, the recurrent hamstring injury re-appeared and forced her to withdraw from the heptathlon, but she still managed to win the Olympic bronze in the long jump.

Jackie Joyner-Kersee is known as one of the greatest female athletes of all time. Jackie won three gold, one silver, and two bronze medals over four consecutive Olympic Games, competing in the long jump and heptathlon events. She set world and Olympic records in the heptathlon and the long jump.
Jackie's accomplishments serve as symbols of strength, courage, and hard work to achieve high goals.

Questions for Thought:

1. Jackie overcame a difficult environment growing up to be successful. What difficulties have you been able to overcome?

2. Asthma and injuries plagued Jackie, but she never gave up. What do you do when you feel like giving up?

3. Jackie stayed away from drugs and alcohol. What effect do you think drugs or alcohol would have on reaching your goals?

Lolo Jones

Backbone of Steel

Photo by Spencer Allen

Lori (Lolo) Jones has overcome many hurdles in her life to excel in track and field. Lolo was raised by a single mother with five children while her father spent most of her childhood in prison. Her family was poor and had to move often, once even living in a church basement. As she entered high school, she parted ways with her mother and stayed with four different families throughout her time in high school. Her high school career drew the attention of Louisiana State University, where Lolo developed into one of the best collegiate hurdlers in the country, becoming a multi-time NCAA champion.

In 2004, Lolo ran in the Olympic Trials but failed to make the Olympic team. As she contemplated her future she knew she would have to make sacrifices and work several part-time jobs in order to make it work financially. But her heart was still in track and field

She entered the 2008 Olympic Games as a favorite and opened a slight lead in the finals of the 100-meter hurdles. With only two hurdles remaining, Lolo was just a few meters from Olympic gold. She was just a couple of seconds from accomplishing her lifetime dream. However, tragedy struck on the next to last hurdle as she tripped and stumbled, dropping to seventh place.

She would have to wait four more years for another opportunity. The pain lasted for months, but Lolo would only use it for motivation to fuel the fire to overcome the hurdles to return to the Olympics.

The tripping over the last hurdle at the 2008 Olympics was attributed to a spinal problem where Lolo couldn't feel her feet. The doctor said the problem was that since she couldn't feel her feet; her brain wasn't able to process where her feet were. The surgery repaired a very painful tethered spinal cord.

With the surgery only a year before the 2012 Olympics, Lolo overcame the odds to come back and qualified for the 2012 Olympic team by placing third at the Olympic Trials. Lolo Jones came all the way back to make the Olympic 100-meter hurdle final again and finished fourth against an outstanding field.

Questions for Thought:

1. Lolo overcame a difficult childhood to be successful. How can you use her story for motivation?

2. Lolo thought about giving up track at one time, but her heart was still in it. How does heart factor into success?

3. Lolo overcame the odds to return to the Olympics. What odds have you overcome?

Francie Larrieu Smith

Five-Time Olympian

Francie Larrieu Smith ran for the San Jose Cindergals, one of the first youth track clubs for women. She graduated before any high school in California fielded a girls' track and field team, so she trained with the boys' team. Her oldest brother, Ron, competed in the 1964 Olympic Games in Tokyo, running in the famous Billy Mills gold medal 10,000-meter race and was an inspiration for Francie that females could accomplish the same thing.

Francie started her career as an 800-meter runner, because at that time that was the longest race in the Olympics for women. In 1972, the women's 1500-meter run was added to the Olympics and Francie moved up to the 1500 meters and finished 8th in the semi-final but failed to make the final. She again made the team in 1976 at 1500 meters and finished 9th in the semi-finals but did not make the final. She made her third Olympic team in 1980, but the U.S. boycotted the Moscow Olympics and Francie missed an opportunity to display her abilities.

She failed to make the 1984 team, but in 1988, the 10,000 meters was added to the Olympics. She planned to compete in both the marathon and 10,000 meters in the 1988 Olympic Trials, but an injury forced her to focus only on the 10,000 meters. She had her highest Olympic finish that year, finishing fifth in 31:35.52.

After 1988, she focused on the marathon and ran a personal best of 2:27.35. She made her fifth Olympic team in 1992 at the age of 39 in the marathon, where she finished 12th and she held the distinct honor of being the flag bearer for the U.S. team for the opening ceremonies.

During a 30-year career that spanned four decades, she established 35 U.S. records and 12 world records in distances ranging from 1000 to 10,000 meters. She was selected by Runner's World magazine as "The Most Versatile Runner of the Quarter Century." Her five Olympic teams established her as an American running legend.

Questions for Thought:

1. Francie Larrieu made five Olympic teams. Imagine how difficult it is to make one Olympic team. What would it take to make five?

2. Francie saw her brother achieve success and realized that females could do it also. How much of accomplishing a task is mental?

3. Women were denied opportunities to run longer distances because some felt they couldn't handle it. How have women proved they can be successful in endurance events?

Jearl Miles-Clark

Five Olympic Teams

Jearl Miles-Clark grew up in Archer, Florida, and started running track because she admired her older sister who ran. In high school, she was competing in the jumps when Alabama A&M track and field coach Joe Henderson recruited her to be a long jumper. However, once she began training at Alabama A&M, a NCAA Division II school, coach Henderson noticed her running ability and placed her in a relay when one of the regular relay members was injured. That would be the start of a long and illustrious running career.

She made the 1988 U.S. Olympic team as an alternate in the 400-meter run. She made her second Olympic team in 1992 in the 400 and 4x400-meter relay and helped the relay team to a silver medal. She finished fifth in the 400-meter semifinals. As Jearl continued to focus on training hard, eating right, and staying drug free, she continued to improve, becoming the No. 1 ranked 400-meter runner in the world in 1993. In 1996, she was fifth in the Olympic Games 400 meters and also anchored the winning 4x400-meter relay.

She continued to run the 400 meters but also started to run the 800 meters and enjoyed immense success. In 1999, she set the American record of 1:56.40 for 800 meters that still stands today.

She made her fourth Olympic team in 2000, qualifying in the 400 and 800 as well as the 4x400-meter relay. She decided to give up her spot in the 400 meters to concentrate on the 800 meters at the Olympics. In the Olympic Trials 800 meters, she joined with her sisters-in-law, Hazel Clark and Joetta Clark-Diggs, to go 1-2-3 to make it a family affair 800-meter team at the Olympics. In Sydney, she suffered from the flu and barely missed the final. She ran the first leg of the 4x400-meter winning relay, which was later stripped of its gold medal when Marion Jones was suspended for drug use.

She came back at age 37 for her fifth Olympics in 2004 more determined than ever. She won the Olympic Trials 800 meters and led the Olympic 800 final, taking the field through the first half in 56.37, but eventually fading to sixth place.

In a career recognized for its excellence as well as its longevity, Jearl Miles-Clark achieved tremendous success in both the 400 and 800 meters. Her ability to challenge from the front or sit-and-kick came from her experience at the top of the world's elite running stage.

Questions for Thought:

1. Jearl moved out of her comfort zone to move up to the 800. Are you stuck in your comfort zone?

2. What are some things you could do to move out of your comfort zone?

3. In her last Olympics, Jearl wasn't afraid to lay it on the line, going out aggressively. Do you go aggressively after your goals?

Madeline Mims

Making the Most of an Opportunity

Madeline Manning Mims won her first national title in the 440-yard run at the girls' A.A.U. Championships while she was a student at John Hay High School in Cleveland in 1956. She went on to Tennessee State University and was a member of the famous Tigerbelles.

Madeline was one of the first female American middle distance stars of world-class caliber. However, early in her career, there were no Olympic events in her specialty. The 800 meters was not an Olympic event for women from 1932 until 1960. In the 1928 Olympics in Amsterdam, several female 800-meter runners collapsed to their knees in exhaustion at the finish line, so the 800 was deemed too exhausting for females. The race did not appear in the Olympics again until 1960 in Rome. In fact, there were no Olympic races farther than 200 meters for women until this time.

Photo Courtesy of USATF

With the 800 meters back in the Olympics, Madeline became the first American to win the event at the 1968 Olympics at Mexico City. She was not expected to win in Mexico City, but upset the field in a decisive victory by more than 10 meters in an Olympic record of 2:00.9. From 1967 to 1980, Madeline won 10 national indoor and outdoor titles and set numerous American records as well. After setting a national record of 2:02.3 in 1967, she improved on that record three times, eventually running 1:57.9. She set three world indoor records, culminating with a best of 2:02.0 in the 800 meters. She also was a member of the 1972 and 1976 Olympic teams and in 1980, at age 32, she won the U.S. Olympic Trials to make her fourth Olympic team. Unfortunately, the U.S. boycott of the Moscow Games kept her out of her fourth Olympics.

Madeline Manning Mims was one of the greatest middle distance runners in U.S. history. Once women regained the right to run distances over 200 meters in the Olympics, Madeline stepped up to make the most of her opportunity.

Questions for Thought:

1. Why didn't Madeline have an opportunity to compete in her best events early in her career?

2. If you are denied an opportunity, what do you do?

3. How do you make the most of your opportunities?

Maria Mutola

Training to be the Best

Maria Mutola grew up in Mozambique excelling in football playing in a boys' league. She began training for track when she was 15 years of age. Not used to the intensive training, Maria initially decided that running was not for her, but was persuaded to continue when it became obvious that she had tremendous potential. After only a few months' training, she won a silver medal in the 800 meters at the African Championships. At the age of 15, she competed in the 1988 Summer Olympics, running a personal best time of 2:04.36, but finishing last in her first round heat.

Over the next few years, Maria failed to improve significantly. She won the African Championships, but faced little opposition in Mozambique and only trained properly when it was the time for big competitions. Her big opportunity came as part of the International Olympic Committee Solidarity Program, when she went to Springfield High School in Oregon to study and train. At the time, Maria spoke no English, but she accepted the challenge. She was a surprise fourth in the final of the 1991 World Championships in Tokyo, where her time of 1:57.63 set a junior world record.

At the 1992 Summer Olympics, Maria hoped to win Mozambique's first Olympic medal. She ran strongly but faded badly in the home straight, eventually finishing fifth. Over the next few years, Maria dominated the 800 meters, winning three world championships and breaking the world record for 1000 meters both indoors and outdoors. At the 1996 Summer Olympics in Atlanta, Maria was the favorite to win the gold, as she hadn't been beaten in an 800-meter race since 1992 and won over 40 consecutive races of 800 and 1000-meter finals. However, suffering from the flu, she ended up finishing third.

Maria won another world indoor championship only weeks after her father had been killed in a car accident. Her greatest moment came at the Sydney Olympics in 2000, when Maria finally won Olympic gold. She returned to Mozambique after her Olympic victory, with huge crowds to cheer her on, and a road was even named in her honor.

Maria returned to the 2004 Olympics in Athens, her fifth Olympics, with a goal of becoming the first woman to successfully defend the Olympic 800-meter title. With dogged determination, Maria was leading until the final few meters when three athletes passed her and she ended up finishing fourth. In her sixth and final Olympic Games in 2008, she finished fifth in the 800 meters and called an end to her 21-year running career.

Questions for Thought:

1. When Maria came to the U.S., she could not even speak English, but she know she would have a better training program. Are you willing to step outside of your comfort zone?

2. Maria sought better training in order to reach her potential. Are you training up to your potential? Why or why not?

3. Maria entered races confident and expecting to win. How do you enter your competitions?

Merlene Ottey

Queen of the Track

Merlene Ottey's inspiration in track and field came from listening to the track and field broadcast from the 1976 Summer Olympics in Montreal, where fellow Jamaican Donald Quarrie ran in the sprint finals. After frequently competing barefooted in local races, she came to the United States to attend the University of Nebraska and compete in track and field.

Merlene began her Olympic career in the 1980 Moscow games and became the first female English-speaking Caribbean athlete to win an Olympic medal, winning bronze at 200 meters. It was the start of her seven Olympic appearances from 1980 to 2004, the most by any track and field athlete in history.

She won an amazing nine Olympic medals (more than any other female athlete), and at the age of 40, became the oldest Olympic medalist in track and field history, winning a silver medal in the 4x100-meter relay. Her 14 world championship medals are more than any other athlete, male or female. Her running resume includes the first woman to run the 60-meter dash in under 7 seconds, the first woman to run the 100-meter dash under 11 seconds, and the first woman in the indoor 200-meter dash to run under 22 seconds. She held the world indoor record at 200 meters for more than 20 years. At one point, Merlene won 57 consecutive 100-meter races and 34 consecutive 200-meter races.

Her Olympic medal haul stands at three silver and six bronze medals. She never won an Olympic gold medal, but narrowly lost by five-thousandths of a second to Gail Devers in the 100-meter final at the 1996 Summer Olympics in Atlanta.

Merlene Ottey competed for the country of Slovenia in the 2004 Olympics and attempted to reach her eighth Olympics, the 2008 Games in Beijing, at the age of 48. She came within 0.28 seconds of making the Olympic team.

Questions for Thought:

1. Merlene made seven Olympic teams. What are the keys to being successful for a long period of time?

2. Merlene loved to compete. Do you love to compete? Why or why not?

3. On a scale of 1-10 (10 high), rate how good of a competitor you are.

Tidye Pickett/Louise Stokes Fraser

Qualified But Not Allowed to Run

Tidye Pickett was a high school track star in Chicago. Louise Stokes Fraser tied the world record in the standing long jump at 8-5¾ as a junior in high school. Both women qualified for the Olympic Trials in 1932, held in Evanston, Illinois. Louise finished third and Tidye tied for fourth in the 100 meters; therefore, qualifying both women for the 4x100-meter relay for the Olympics to be held in Los Angeles. The women made history as the first two African American women to qualify for an Olympic team.

When the Olympic team stopped for lodging on the way to the Olympics in Los Angeles, Stokes and Pickett were given a room separate from the rest of the team and were served dinner in their rooms, rather than with the team at a banquet. At the Olympic Games, coach George Vreeland selected only white women for the final relay team, which went on to win the gold medal in world record time. Having beaten the women selected ahead of them, the discrimination was a crushing blow for Tidye and Louise.

Tidye and Louise both used the disappointment of not getting to compete as motivation to qualify again in 1936 for the Olympics. Tidye made the Olympic team by finishing second in the 80-meter hurdles at the Olympic Trials. Louise placed fifth in the 100 meters and again made the Olympic team as a member of the 4x100-meter relay team. Proud of their native hero, Louise's hometown of Chicago raised the money to send her to Berlin. However, after arriving in Berlin, Louise was stunned to learn a white runner had once again replaced her, and the team went on to win the gold medal.

Tidye did get to compete in the 1936 Olympic Games, running the 80-meter hurdles to become the first African American to compete in the Olympic Games. Unfortunately, Tidye broke her foot racing in the Olympics.

Both runners had their Olympic careers ended when World War II caused the cancellation of the Olympics in 1940 and 1944. Tidye Pickett and Louise Stokes Fraser made history as the first two African American women to make the U.S. Olympic team. Their pioneering efforts opened the door for many young women to follow.

Questions for Thought:

1. Louise and Tidye felt like they were better than the two runners selected to run ahead of them. How would you react to this situation?

2. Both women faced racial and gender discrimination. Do you feel like you have ever been discriminated against?

3. What can you do to help stop or prevent discrimination on your team?

Ana Fidelia Quirot

I Will Run Again

Growing up, Ana Quirot had two heroes: Fidel Castro, the dictator of Cuba, and Cuban running legend Alberto Juantorena, who won gold medals in the 400 and 800 meter races at the 1976 Olympics. Ana was overweight as a girl, but lost weight when she began running seriously as a teen. At the age of 13, she was accepted into one of Cuba's prestigious state sports schools and began seriously training.

Ana found her niche in the 400 and 800 meters. Just as Ana was beginning to reach her peak performance years, the Cuban government decided to boycott the 1984 and 1988 Olympics Games. Ana's chance to prove herself on the international level came in the late 1980s and early 1990s. In 1989 she turned in an undefeated year in the 800-meter race. Her string of 39 consecutive victories in the 800 meters led to her being chosen as the I.A.A.F.'s female athlete of the year.

In the early weeks of a pregnancy, Ana ran the 800 meters in 1:56.80 for a bronze medal at the 1992 Summer Olympics in Barcelona, Spain. Ana was on top of the world, as she was widely admired for her beauty as well as her talent. In her seventh month of pregnancy, Ana was preparing to launder her clothes using a small kerosene-powered cook stove when an explosion occurred. In seconds, Ana was engulfed in a fire that burnt 38 percent of her body and brought her to the verge of death. She passed in and out of shock as her system reacted to the burns. Her baby, born prematurely, died. Scars on her face and neck marred her once-legendary beauty. When Ana regained consciousness in a hospital burn unit, Fidel Castro was standing at her bedside. "I will run again," she told him.

Ana faced a very lengthy recovery period, involving numerous skin-graft operations. To the amazement of medical experts, less than four months after the fire, she was back on the track. Ana's ability to move was restricted by the scar tissue on her stomach, arms, and hands. Her training time was restricted to the early morning and late evening hours when the sun could not hurt her damaged skin. Despite a scarred body, the fighting spirit of Ana Quirot still soared.

Ana was 29 years old when the accident occurred and was in the height of her career. She missed the 1994 track season due to a dozen rounds of plastic surgery. In 1995 she won the world championship at 800 meters, and the following year in the 1996 Olympic Games, she just missed winning the gold, capturing a silver medal. Ana Quirot's dramatic struggle to overcome adversity has turned her into a mythological hero in her own country.

Questions for Thought:

1. Despite being near death, Ana never gave up and overcame the odds. Think of a time you overcame the odds to accomplish a goal.

2. Ana was on top of the world until her accident. How do you think you would have reacted to the accident?

3. Ana recovered very quickly because of her positive attitude. How does attitude affect recovery?

Paula Radcliffe

Resolve to Succeed

Born in England, Paula Radcliffe started running at the age of 7 despite suffering asthma and anemia. Her first race at a national level came as a 12-year-old in 1986 when she placed 299th out of 600 runners in the English Schools Cross Country Championships. One year later, she finished fourth in the same race.

Paula won the 1992 World Junior Cross Country titles and continued to improve. She made the 1996 British Olympic team at 5000 meters in the 1996 Olympic Games in Atlanta and placed fifth.

She made the British Olympic team for the 2000 Olympics in the 5000 meters and set a new British record. However, three runners sprinted ahead of Paula near the end of the race and kept her out of the medals as she finished fourth. In 2002, she moved up to the marathon, running a world record time of 2:17:18 in the Chicago Marathon, later lowering that to 2:15:25 in 2003.

Paula was the favorite to win a gold medal in the 2004 Olympic Games in Athens. However, two weeks prior to the Olympic marathon, she suffered a leg injury. The resulting use of anti-inflammatory drugs had an adverse effect on her stomach. Visibly in pain, Paula kept giving everything she had in order to get through the race, desperately trying to take in every last drop of her carbohydrate drinks from the drink stations along the way. After struggling for over two hours of the marathon run, Paula finally had to withdraw. Five days later, she had to withdraw partway through the 10,000 meters. They were the first races Paula had to withdraw from and she suffered from extreme distress in what she called the worst moment of her career.

Despite a commitment to returning to the Olympics in 2008, she was persistently bothered by injuries, including a stress fracture and a foot injury. She battled back to compete in the 2008 Olympics, but had severe cramps during the Olympic marathon that slowed her to a 23rd place finish. Again, she focused on the 2012 Olympics, but was forced to withdraw before the competition began due to a foot injury.

Paula became a passionate spokesperson against drug cheats. Inspired by her own battle with asthma, she is widely admired for her work in asthma research. Paula is considered one of the best female distance runners never to win an Olympic medal, but with great pride, she has kept an eternally positive manner and tough resolve to succeed.

Questions for Thought:

1. Paula's failures have just served to motivate her more. How could failure help to motivate you?

2. What does the phrase "the greater the challenge, the greater the reward" mean to you?

3. Paula is an advocate of drug free competition. How strong of a stand are you willing to take on drug cheating?

Sanya Richards-Ross

Rough Road to Gold

Sanya Richards-Ross won 10 individual gold medals in the Florida High School State Track and Field Championships in the 100, 200, and 400 meters, and long jump, and also added a team gold in the 4x100-meter relay. Her team won four straight state team titles and she set the Florida state record for 400 meters. Her senior year, she was honored as the national track and field female high school athlete of the year. Her freshman year at the University of Texas, she was the NCAA national champion in both the 400 meters and 4x400-meter relay. As a sophomore, she anchored her team to a 4x400 relay title and won the 400 meters, setting a national collegiate record in the indoor 400 meters. At the conclusion of her sophomore year at the University of Texas, Sanya turned professional in track and field but continued to attend classes at Texas.

Photo by Spencer Allen

She competed in the 2004 Athens Olympics, finishing sixth in the 400 meters, and ran on the gold medal-winning 4x400-meter relay team. Sanya became the youngest woman to ever run under 49 seconds in the women's 400 meters, breaking the American record with a time of 48.70.

In 2006, Sanya was undefeated in the outdoor track and field season. However, in 2007, just a year before the Olympics, she was struggling with an illness that prevented her from running at her peak. She had to withdraw from several meets because she suffered from Behcet's Syndrome, a rare disease of the immune system, which causes painful body sores.

Sanya persevered and recovered to enter the Beijing Olympics as the favorite to win the gold medal. She went out very strong at the start of the race and opened up a commanding lead; however, she faltered in the homestretch and was passed by Christine Ohuruogu of Great Britain and had to settle for the bronze medal. Sanya got a chance for redemption a few days later in the 4x400-meter relay. After the first three runners, the United States was in second place and trailed Russia by two meters. Sanya, the anchor leg, kicked into a different gear and furiously began pursuing the Russian runner. Sanya's determination helped her catch the Russian runner with 30 meters to go to give the U.S. the gold medal.

At the 2012 London Olympics on August 5, 2012, Sanya overtook the competition in the last 40 meters to win the coveted gold medal in the women's 400 meters in 49.55. Sanya also anchored the gold medal-winning U.S. women's 4x400-meter relay team. Through hard work and persistence to fight through injuries, Sanya Richards-Ross she has been a positive role model for women.

Questions for Thought:

1. Sanya did 1000 sit-ups every day! What special commitment are you willing to make?

2. What are some barriers that limit you in reaching your potential?

3. How could you overcome those barriers?

Louise Ritter

Overcoming Childhood Roadblocks

Louise Ritter's athletic career hit a roadblock at age 9 when she contracted rheumatic fever and was prohibited from any strenuous activity for almost three years. After her recovery, she established herself as a premier athlete, high jumping 5-11½, the second highest high jump in the nation as a high school sophomore, in 1976.

When she enrolled at Texas Women's University in 1977, she was persuaded to change her style from the straddle to the Fosbury Flop, and her career soared to new heights. While attending Texas Woman's University, she captured national titles three out of four years and set her first American record at age 20. Louise held the American record on 10 different occasions, competed on three United States Olympic teams and was the premier women's high jumper in the United States for a decade from 1979 to 1989.

Despite her great success, her career was far from smooth sailing. Complications from injuries affected her jumping and she was forced to have arthroscopic knee surgery in 1983 and 1985, and in 1984 she injured her hip. Louise had a disappointing performance at the 1984 Olympics Games in Los Angeles, finishing eighth with a best jump of 6-3.

Entering the 1988 Olympic Games in Seoul, South Korea, the overwhelming favorite for the gold medal was world record holder Stefka Kostadinova of Bulgaria. Louise and Kostadinova were the only two jumpers to clear 6-7 in the competition and were tied for the lead. The bar went to 6-8 and they both missed all three attempts at that height. The rules in this situation call for a jump-off starting with one additional jump at the last height they both missed. Kostadinova missed her first jump of the jump-off and Louise followed by clearing the bar to equal her national record and secure the gold medal, becoming the first American woman to win a high jump gold medal in the Olympics in more than 50 years.

Questions for Thought:

1. Louise Ritter was prohibited for doing strenuous activity for three years. What would your life be like if you had to eliminate all strenuous activity?

2. Do you ever take your physical ability and the opportunities you have to engage in physical activities for granted?

3. Louise Ritter was a very successful athlete. How do you encourage others that may not be having as much success as you?

Betty Robinson

First Female Olympic Gold Medalist

At age 16, American Betty Robinson competed in her first 100-meter race ever and finished second to the American record holder. In her second race ever, she equaled the world record for the 100 meters. Her third competition was the Olympic Trials, where she made the Olympic team. The 1928 Olympic Games was only her fourth competition, as she had only been running for four months.

The Amsterdam Olympics in 1928 was the first year that women were allowed to compete in the Olympic Games. Wearing a skirt, Betty lined up for the first women's Olympic final ever, the 100-meter dash. Betty sprinted to the win, equaling the world record and becoming the inaugural gold medal winner for women. She also added a silver medal as a member of the 4x100 meter relay team.

Tragedy struck in 1931 when Betty was severely injured in a plane crash. She was dragged from the wreckage with a severe concussion, a crushed arm, and a broken leg. A passerby mistook her for dead and drove her to the mortuary. Doctors gave her a slim chance of survival, let alone of walking again. She was in a coma for seven weeks, in a wheelchair for six months, and it took her two years before she could walk normally again.

While she was recuperating from her injuries, she missed an opportunity to compete before the home crowd at the 1932 Olympic Games in Los Angeles. With fierce determination, Betty battled back to make the 1936 Olympic team. Although unable to bend her knee for a crouching start in the 100 meters, she earned a spot running the third leg on the U.S. 4x100-meter relay team. The U.S. team was running behind the favored German team when the Germans dropped the baton and the U.S. went on to win.

For Betty Robinson, it was a remarkable rise, fall, and rise again; however, the damaged leg resulting from the crash robbed her of her peak years. But, by crossing the line first in Amsterdam years earlier, she guaranteed her place in the history books.

Questions for Thought:

1. Betty Robinson was a pioneer. Imagine what it would have felt like to be the very first person to win an Olympic gold medal.

2. How did Betty pave the way for future generations to come?

3. Betty struggled for years to return after injuries to compete again. What does that fierce determination say about a person? How do actions speak louder than words?

Wilma Rudolph

The Black Gazelle

Wilma Rudolph's race in life started very slowly as the 20th of 22 children. She was born prematurely and weighed only 4.5 pounds at birth. Because of racial segregation, Wilma and her mother were not permitted to be cared for at the local hospital because it was for whites only. The only black doctor was 50 miles away, which was a hardship on the Rudolph family's budget. Through the next several years, Wilma faced one hardship after another in the form of measles, mumps, scarlet fever, chicken pox, and double pneumonia.

When Wilma was 6 years old, it was discovered that her left leg and foot were becoming weak and deformed with polio, a crippling disease that had no cure. The doctor told Wilma that she would never walk again. Wilma and her mother were determined not to give up. With the help of the black medical college of Fisk University in Nashville, Wilma went through vigorous physical therapy using crutches, braces, and corrective shoes. Finally, by the age of 12, she could walk normally and decided to become an athlete.

In high school Wilma became a basketball star, setting state records for scoring and leading her team to the state championship. By the time she was 16, she earned a berth on the U.S. Olympic track and field team and came home from the 1956 Melbourne Games with an Olympic bronze medal in the 4x100 meter relay.

At the 1960 Summer Olympics in Rome, 80,000 spectators filled the Olympic Stadium in temperatures over 100 degrees. In the 100 meters, she tied the world record of 11.3 in the semifinals and then won the final in 11.0. However, because of a 2.75-meter per second wind, above the acceptable limit of two meters per second, she didn't receive credit for a world record. In the 200 meters, she broke the Olympic record in the opening heat in 23.2 and won the final in 24.0. In the 4x100-meter relay, Wilma, despite a poor baton pass, overtook Germany's anchor leg and the Americans, all women from Tennessee State, took the gold in 44.5 after setting a world record of 44.4 in the semifinals.

Wilma did more than promote her country. In her soft-spoken, gracious manner, she paved the way for future African American athletes, both men and women.

Questions for Thought:

1. Wilma Rudolph could not walk normally until she was 12, yet four years later, she was on the Olympic team. Do you ever think something is impossible?

2. Wilma was gracious and humble as an athlete. On a scale of 1-10 (10 high), how humble are you?

3. How does the Wilma Rudolph story inspire you?

Marla Runyan

Overcoming Obstacles

When Marla Runyan was in the fourth grade, she first noticed that something was wrong with her vision, because she couldn't see the chalkboard at school very clearly. She also had trouble reading her books. Her condition was diagnosed as Stargardt disease, a degenerative disorder that is the most common cause of blindness in the United States. Her vision later deteriorated to 20/300 in the left eye and 20/400 in the right eye, making her legally blind.

Marla competed in gymnastics and soccer until she just couldn't see the ball anymore. She then started participating in track and field, where she excelled in the high jump in high school and picked up the heptathlon in college at San Diego State University. She placed 10th at the 1996 Olympic Trials in the heptathlon and broke the heptathlon 800-meter record in 2:04.70, convincing her to drop the heptathlon and train for the middle distance events. She disappeared from the track scene for two years after the trials, having a knee surgery and a foot surgery.

Despite seeing only blurs and shadows when she runs, which makes it difficult to run in a pack, Marla succeeded at the highest level. In 2000, she became the first legally blind athlete to compete in the Olympic Games, making the Olympic final and finishing eighth in the 5000 meters. She also broke the U.S. indoor track record for the 5000 meters by running 15:07.33. In 2002, Marla was the top United States female in the 5000 meters and the marathon.

Marla Runyan refused to use her blindness as an excuse. The story of her will to succeed is motivation for future generations.

Questions for Thought:

1. What obstacles did Marla Runyan overcome?

2. How difficult do you believe it would be to run if you were legally blind?

3. What can you do when you feel sorry for yourself?

Kate Schmidt

Kate the Great

Kate Schmidt was lucky to grow up in California, the mecca of javelin throwing during the 1960s. At the age of 13, she took up the sport, and a year later, she almost made the U.S. Olympic team. When Kate was just 15, she won the U.S. national championship. In 1972, she won the U.S. Olympic Trials and won a bronze medal at the Munich Olympic Games. Four years later, she duplicated the feat, winning the Olympic Trials and capturing another bronze in the 1976 Montreal Olympic Games.

Kate was denied the opportunity to compete in 1980 when she was a member of the boycotting 1980 Olympics team. In 1984, she just missed making the games after finishing fourth in the qualifying trials.

Kate sustained many injuries throughout her career and spent numerous hours in the pool cross training. Kate's discovery that water was a natural and effective healer interested her, and she went on to develop water rehabilitation techniques based on basic physical therapy principles.

Kate "The Great" Schmidt was one of the greatest U.S. female javelin throwers ever. She won the national Amateur Athletic Union championships seven times between 1969 and 1979, winning two bronze medals in the Olympics and improved the U.S. record several times, finishing with a world record of 227-5 in 1977.

Questions for Thought:

1. Kate took her discovery of the healing powers of water and developed new training methods. How can cross training make you a better athlete?

2. When injured, you lose your mental confidence quicker than you lose your physical fitness. How can you maintain your confidence when injured?

3. How might an injury help you to improve in another aspect of your training?

Janelle Smith (Carson)

Pioneer Sprinter

In the early 1960s, Janelle Smith's high school in the small town of Fredonia, Kansas, didn't have a girls' track team. Janelle ran against the boys. Her father, Meade Smith, was her coach. Meade was an outstanding sprinter who was invited to the 1936 Olympic Trials, but unfortunately, didn't have the money to attend.

Janelle started winning U.S. Junior Olympic Championships when she was 11. In 1961, as a high school freshman, she posted one of the top 100-yard dash times in the nation. She could long jump 19-0, run the 220-yard dash in 24.0, and the 100-yard dash in 10.8. She set Junior Olympic records galore. As a high school student, she made several U.S. national teams, competing in the 100 and 200 meters while getting valuable international competition experience.

Though she was among the two or three fastest girls in the nation at 100 meters, she realized that with hard work and proper training she could develop and utilize her stamina to run longer races. Her dad encouraged her to move up to the 400 meters.

The move up to the 400 meters proved to be highly successful. As a high school senior, Janelle won the 1964 Olympic trials at 400 meters and qualified for the 1964 Olympic Games in Tokyo, Japan. She did not qualify for the 400-meter final, but in the semifinals of the 1964 Games, she set an American record of 54.5. In 1965, Janelle lowered her American 400-meter record to 53.7 and appeared on the cover of the May 10, 1965 issue of Sports Illustrated.

After the Olympics, Janelle attended Emporia State Teachers College, which had yet to form a women's track team. Despite having to overcome the challenge of not having organized girls track in high school and college, Janelle Smith used her talent and dedication to a become a pioneer and role model for women.

Questions for Thought:

1. When you are denied an opportunity, how do you make the best of it?

2. What support do you have in place to help you succeed?

3. If you were successful in one event, would you be willing to change events if you knew you had to work harder, but it was an opportunity for you to be great?

Helen Stephens

The Fulton Flash

Helen Stephens was born in Fulton, Missouri, and acquired the nickname "the Fulton Flash." As a child, she loved to run, jump, and climb. She also had to work hard on the family farm. She attended Fulton High School and dreamed of being the fastest girl in the world, but the school did not have athletic teams for girls. Fortunately, her high school physical education teacher, Burton Moore, knew about track and field training.

A few days after her 17th birthday, coach Moore took Helen to her first official race. She ran against the reigning Olympic 100-meter champion Stella Walsh, from Poland. Helen beat Walsh in the indoor 50 meters in world record time.

At age 18, she competed in the 1936 Olympics in Berlin, Germany, winning the 100 meters. Her time of 11.5 was a world record that stood for 24 years. She came back to anchor the U.S. 4x100-meter relay team that won the Olympic title in a world record time of 46.9. She also competed in the throwing events, finishing ninth in the discus at the 1936 Olympics.

Her career lasted less than three years, but it involved more than 100 races, and she won them all.

After the Olympics, she turned professional and ran exhibition races against Jesse Owens. For seven years she toured with two professional basketball teams, becoming the first woman to create, own, and manage her own semiprofessional basketball team.

Helen Stephens was a tremendous competitor who never lost a race. She helped pave the way for future female athletes.

Questions for Thought:

1. Helen loved sports, but her school did not have women's athletics. How courageous were the female pioneers who helped pave the way for future women?

2. Helen never lost a race. What are some attributes that would make that possible?

3. Helen's success continued after her running days were over. How would a successful athletic career transfer into a successful career?

Katherine Switzer

Pushing Back

Katherine Switzer was born in Virginia and attended Syracuse University. While at Syracuse, Katherine entered and completed the Boston Marathon in 1967, finishing in 4:20:00. During that time period, the idea of women running the 26.2-mile distance was so foreign, the rulebook made no mention of them. Even though the rulebook did not specifically state women could not run, women were not welcome to run the Boston Marathon. A prevailing attitude was that women could not run long distances without doing their bodies harm. So Katherine tried to keep a low profile and registered under the name "K.V. Switzer."

When race director Jock Semple realized a woman was entering the race, he attempted to remove her from the race physically by tearing off her bib number. Katherine's boyfriend was running with her and shoved Semple aside, allowing Katherine to finish the race. As Katherine was running the final miles of the marathon, she vowed she would work to create running opportunities for all women. After that race, The Amateur Athletic Union immediately barred women from all competition with male runners. Despite the protest from women, it took five years until women were officially welcome to run the Boston Marathon in 1972, the same year Title IX became law.

Katherine trained as many as 110 miles per week. She won the New York City Marathon in 1974 and claimed a personal best time of 2:51.37 at the Boston Marathon. After her running career was over, she became a tireless crusader to promote women's marathon running and was a prime advocate for the Olympics to include a women's marathon in the 1984 Olympic Games.

Katherine's courage to run the Boston Marathon paved the way for generations of women runners to live their dreams. Her efforts created a social revolution by empowering women around the world through running. Ever since Katherine Switzer was pushed in the Boston Marathon, she has fought back, and women distance runners will be forever grateful.

Questions for Thought:

1. Why should women distance runners be grateful for the efforts of Katherine Switzer?

2. How have women proved they are capable of grueling endurance feats?

3. Katherine had the courage to fight for her rights. How have you fought for what you believe to be right?

Gwen Torrence

Tough Competitor

Gwen Torrence spent the first few days of her life in an incubator, as she was born with the umbilical cord around her neck. She grew up in subsidized housing projects and first started attracting attention from her physical education teacher when he noticed her speed and wanted her to come out for track. It took a while for Gwen to overcome her shyness to join the team and initially she only practiced after the other girls had gone home. She won three consecutive state 100 and 200-meter dash state championships and also won two gold medals at the National Junior Olympics.

Gwen was offered a scholarship at Georgia University, which she initially refused. Gwen saw no need to attend college since she planned to become a hairstylist, but her high school coach finally convinced her a college degree was important and she became the first in her family to go to college.

Her workouts at Georgia were legendary. She drove herself to work harder and longer than others despite the oppressive Georgia heat. She made herself into a top competitor. At Georgia, she won four NCAA titles and had an opportunity to compete at the 1984 U.S. Olympics Trials, but she declined because she was too nervous.

After graduating from Georgia, she turned professional and won 33 consecutive races, becoming a favorite for the 1988 Olympics. Gwen made the 100-meter final and finished in fifth place.

With support from her family, she set her sights on the 1992 Olympics. She won her first Olympic gold medal in the 200 meters, and also won gold in the 4x100-meter relay and silver in the 4x400-meter relay. After finishing fourth in the 100 meters, she was outspoken, suspecting that two of the three medalists had used banned substances. She did not name names, which drew a hail of criticism from the news media and the wrath of some of her competitors.

With the 1996 Olympic Games coming to her hometown area, (she lived in an Atlanta housing project, 10 minutes from the Olympic Stadium, until she was 4 years old) the pressure began to build off of being an Olympic star in her hometown. Competing in her third Olympic Games, she won bronze in the 100 meters and gold in the 4x100 meter relay.

Gwen Torrence will go down in history as one of the best and most versatile women sprinters of all time.

Questions for Thought:

1. Gwen overcame her shyness to be successful. Are there any areas in your life you have to work hard at to overcome deficiencies?

2. Gwen showed her fighting spirit by running. Do you have a fighting spirit? How do you show it?

3. Gwen tried to outwork everyone to become the best. How hard are you willing to work?

Blanka Vlasic

Born to Jump

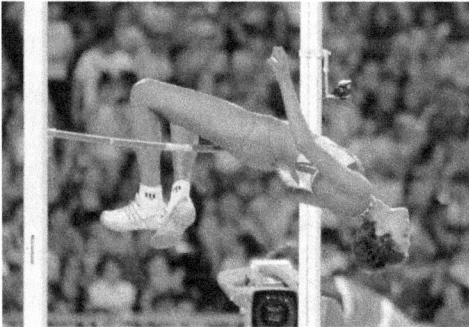

Photo by Pretty Sporty/Cheryl Treworgy

Blanka Vlasic grew up in Croatia, born to parents with an athletic background. Her dad once held the Croation decathlon record. As a child, Blanka would go to the track while her dad practiced. Due to her tall and slender build, she gravitated to the high jump. She jumped 5-10¾ as a 15-year-old and 6-4 as a 16-year-old.

She represented Croatia in the 2000 Olympic Games at age 16, stamping herself as a future star in the high jump by placing 17th. At 19 years of age, she jumped over the magic two meter (6-6¾) barrier, both a physiological and psychological barrier.

She jumped 6-8 to set a Croatian record, which set her up to be a contender for the 2004 Athens Olympics, but she could only manage a jump of 6-2¼ to finish 11th in the 2004 Olympics. Blanka was diagnosed with a hyperthyroid condition, which left her feeling lethargic, and she did not compete for a year after she had surgery.

She came back stronger in 2007, jumping over the two meter barrier (6-6¾) in 17 of her 19 outdoor competitions, and made several close attempts at the world record height of 6-10¾. She was dominant in winning 18 of her 19 outdoor competitions. As the 2008 Olympics approached, Blanka went into the high jump competition with a 34 meet winning streak. She cleared 6-8¾, the same mark as Belgian Tia Hellebaut, but Blanka needed one more attempt and had to settle for the silver.

In 2009, she set her personal best clearing 6-9¾, and tied the second best performance of all-time in the high jump. As one of the most dominant high jumpers in history, Blanka focused on the 2012 Olympic Games. She was the favorite going into 2012, but an operation to repair her Achilles tendon became infected and she was forced to withdraw from the Olympics.

Questions for Thought:

1. Blanka has been one of the most dominant high jumpers ever, but is still missing a gold medal. Is your career defined by how wins you have?

2. Blanka had early success and the high jump came natural to her. How does hard work combine with talent for success?

3. Which is more important in reaching in helping you reach your goal? Talent or work ethic? How could you combine both to reach your maximum potential?

Lauryn Williams

Hard Work Knows No Limits

Photo Courtesy of USATF

Lauryn Williams set records for the 100 and 200 meters, long jump, and 4x100-meter relay during high school; however, she took the sport lightly and trained very little. However, all that changed when Lauryn went to the University of Miami to run track. She reported to the team out of shape and quickly realized if she was going to be successful, she would have to make a commitment. She developed her motto, "Hard work knows no limits." That motto enabled her to progress and be successful at the highest level.

At the 2004 U.S. Olympic Trials, Lauryn's lean at the finish nipped two-time Olympic 100-meter champion Gail Devers to earn the final spot by one one-hundredth of a second. Lauryn's family attended the Olympics to support her, despite her dad needing six dialysis treatments while in Athens.

At 21 years of age and one of the smallest runners in the field at 5-3, Lauryn showed her ability to rise to the challenge at the big meets by capturing second place in the 2004 Olympics at 100 meters.

Lauryn fought off injuries to qualify for the U.S. Olympic team that competed in the 2008 Beijing Games. The U.S. was one of the favorites to win the 4x100-meter relay; however, with Lauryn on the anchor in the semifinal, a dropped baton on her handoff took the U.S. out of the race. Disappointed, Lauryn refocused to finish fourth in the 100-meter final.

Lauryn almost gave up track in the period between the 2008 and 2012 Olympics. A continuous string of injuries and the death of her father left her out of competitions. Fortunately, she returned to the track and her sixth place finish in the 2012 Olympic Trials left her out of an individual event, but she did earn a spot in the 4x100-meter relay pool.

In the 2012 Olympics in London, Lauryn ran the anchor leg of the 4x100-meter relay for U.S. in the qualification round. She was not part of the final where the U.S team went on to win gold and earn a new world record with a time of 40.82, but as a relay team member in the qualifying rounds, she received a gold medal. Lauryn Williams, the small girl with big dreams, came a long way to fulfill her dreams at the top of the sprinting world.

Questions for Thought:

1. What does the motto, "Hard Work Knows No Limits" mean to you?

2. Lauryn was often the smallest competitor in the field. Does your size make a difference in your performance? In your effort?

3. Lauryn returned to track because of her love for the sport. What do you love about your sport?

Fatima Whitbread

Survivor

All success involves overcoming adversity, but Fatima had to battle more than her share. She began life unwanted. Her parents abandoned her as a baby, leaving her in a house alone. She was discovered crying days later by neighbors and had to spend four months in a hospital recovering from malnutrition.

Fatima spent the first 14 years of her life in children's homes in Great Britain. Those years were full of abuse. Social workers tried to develop a relationship between Fatima and her violent birth mother, a hopeless quest that finally ended when her mother's boyfriend raped Fatima at 12 years of age, while her birth mother held a knife to her throat to quiet her down.

She was adopted by the national javelin coach Margaret Whitbread, who discovered she had the talent to be a great javelin thrower. Finally, she had a loving, stable home life, which she had never known before.

Margaret took Fatima to world class success. As a teenager, Fatima won a bronze medal at the 1984 Olympic Games in Los Angeles, despite competing with an illness and against doctors' orders. She set a world record in 1986 with a throw of 254-1 and was the top javelin thrower in the world, winning a world championship in 1987.

Fatima set her sights on the 1988 Olympic Games, but was struck with illness and injury again. Just as in the previous Olympics, doctors advised her not to compete, but she once again went against doctors' orders and she competed and won the silver medal. Fatima suffered a shoulder injury in 1989 and reoccurrences of that injury forced her to retire.

Fatima Whitbread emerged from a horrific childhood to become one of Great Britain's greatest athletes. She defeated her demons and transformed devastating experiences into life lessons that led to triumph against the worst hardships imaginable.

Questions for Thought:

1. Fatima's coach assisted her in achieving her goals. How has someone been there for you to assist you?

2. Fatima had nightmares for years about her childhood abuse. Eventually she became stronger mentally and was able to put her past behind her. How do you use your mental abilities to be successful?

3. Fatima was struck by bad luck twice at the Olympic Games. Can you control luck? What things might you be able to control to increase your chances of success?

Willye White

From the Cotton Fields to Five Time Olympian

Willye White was born in Money, Mississipi, and was raised by her grandparents. She started chopping cotton when she was 10-years-old. She started track as a 10-year-old sprinter, but turned to the long jump because she felt everybody wanted to be a sprinter.

Willye attended college at Tennessee State University, where her teammate was Wilma Rudolph. Willye became the first American track and field athlete to compete in five Olympics, competing in every Olympics from 1956 through 1972. Her first Olympic appearance was as a 16-year-old high school sophomore, when she won a silver medal in the long jump in 1956, marking the first time a U.S woman had ever medaled in that event. She added another silver medal in the 4x100-meter relay in 1964.

For almost two decades, she was America's best female long jumper with a personal best of 21-6, setting seven American records.

Willye grew up before the civil rights movement and overcame all the hurdles she had as an African American woman. She credited her experience as an athlete with allowing her to see beyond the racism and hatred that surrounded her as a child.

Although Willye went through many struggles, she was always willing to give back. She started the Willye White Foundation to raise money for kids in housing projects so that they could go to school. The emphasis of the foundation is equal education and equal rights for everyone.

Questions for Thought:

1. Willye overcame racism to be successful. How can you help to eliminate discrimination?

2. Willye wanted to help those less fortunate. How can you help those less fortunate than you?

3. As a child she had a non-glamorous job of picking cotton. How might that have helped her achieve success?

References

Arnold, C. (2012, February 10). Hassiba Boulmerka: Defying death threats to win gold. *BBC News Magazine*. Retrieved from http://www.bbc.co.uk/news/magazine-16962799

Australians. (n.d.) *Betty Cuthbert. Australians.* Retrieved Dec. 23, 2013 from http://www.abc.net.au/schoolstv/australians/cuthbert.htm

Alice Coachman Track and Field Foundation. (2008, January). Retrieved October 22, 2010, from http://www.alicecoachman.org/

Alice Coachman Biography-Winner at Wembley, Great Olympic Athlete, Awards and Accomplishments, Further Information. (2011). Retrieved September 18, 2010 from http://sports.jrank.org/pages/925/Coachman-Alice.html

Atcheson, C. (2008, July 14). Wyomia Tyus. *SI Vault.* Retrieved from http://sportsillustrated.cnn.com/vault/article/magazine/MAG1141780/index.htm

Babe Didrickson Zaharias. Biography. (n.d) *bio.True Story*. Retrieved from http://www.biography.com/people/babe-didrikson-zaharias-9542047?page=3

Barnette, N.,Woodard,C., Gossett, L. J., Lifford, T. Sams, J. D. (1996). *Run for the Dream: The Gail Devers Story* [Television broadcast].

Benoit-Samuelson, J. (1987). *Running Tide.* New York, NY: Knopf Publishing.

Benyo, R., Henderson, J. (2001). *Running Encyclopedia: The Ultimate Source for Todays Runner.* Champaign, IL: Human Kinetics.

Betty Cuthbert. (n.d*.). Australian Olympic Committee*. Retrieved from http://corporate.olympics.com.au/athlete/betty-cuthbert

Bijkerk, T. (2004, May). Fanny Blankers-Koen. *A Biography Journal of Olympic History,* 12(2), 56–60.

Biracee, T. (1990). *Wilma Rudolph.* Los Angeles, CA: Holloway House Publishing Company.

Blanka Vlasic pulls out of London Games. (2012, July 14). *BBC.* Retrieved December 11, 2012 from http://www.bbc.co.uk/sport/0/olympics/18842591

Vlasic, B. (n.d.) *Blanka Vlasic.* Retrieved on January 7, 2012 from: http://www.blanka-vlasic.hr/n-en.php?id=657

Boyle, R.H. (1965, May 10). Marie Mulder. *SI Vault,* 22. Retrieved September 24, 2010 from http://sportsillustrated.cnn.com/vault/cover/toc/7921/index.htm

Brown, E.D. (n.d.) *Sports Biograpies.* HickockSports.com. Retrieved from http://www.hickoksports.com/biograph/brownear.shtml

Braun, E. (2005). *Wilma Rudolph.* Mankato, MN: Capstone Press.

Brown, Earlene (2009, Feb. 18) Brown, Earlene. *Hickock Sports.* Retrieved January 6, 2013 from: http://www.hickoksports.com/biograph/brownear.shtml

Brown, L. (2012, September 16) Dame Kelly Holmes: I used to cut myself and even though of suicide because the pressure to win was so great. *Daily Mail Online.* Retrieved January 5, 2013 from: http://www.dailymail.co.uk/news/article-2204005/Double-gold-Olympic-medallist-Dame-Kelly-Holmes-reveals-long-battle-self-harming-admits-thought-taking-life.html

Butler, S. (2012, April 12). How Katherine Switzer Paved the Way. *ESPNW.* Retrieved January 5, 20123 from http://espn.go.com/espnw/more-sports/7803502/2012-boston-marathon-how-kathrine-switzer-paved-way-female-runners

Cathy Freeman Foundation. (n.d.). Retrieved September 20, 2010, from http://www. cathyfreemanfoundation.org.au/

Cayleff, S. (1996). *Babe: The Life and Legend of Babe Didrikson Zaharias.* University of Illinois Press.

Cazeneuve, B. (2000, March 6). What's Up? Doc! *SI Vault.* Retrieved January 13, 2013 from http://sportsillustrated.cnn.com/vault/article/magazine/MAG1018457/index.htm

Clark Diggs, J. (2009). *Joetta 's "P" Principles for Success: Life Lessons Learned from Track and Field.* Xlibris.

Davis, M. (1992). *Black American Women in Olympic Track and Field: A Complete Illustrated Reference.* Jefferson, NC: McFarland and Co.

Davis, S. (2005). *A Treadmill Mom Goes for the Gold.* Retrieved January 13, 2012 from http://www.medicinenet.com/script/main/art.asp?articlekey=50923

Evelyn Ashford Biography-Racing The Boys, Chronology, Bitter Disappointment, Double Gold, Gold And Silver, The Fastest Doubleheader Ever (n.d.). Retrieved October 14, 2010 from http://sports.jrank.org/

Fatima Whitbread. (n.d.) *United Kingdom Athletics.* Retrieved from http://www.uka.org.uk/e-inspire/hall-of-fame-athletes/fatima-whitbread/

Flanagan, A. K. (2000). *Wilma Rudolph: Athlete and Educator.* Chicago, Illinois: Ferguson Publishing Company.

Forman, K. (2005). *The Fragile Champion: Doris Brown Who Always Ran the Extra Mile.* Mustang, OK: Tate Publishing.

Freedman, R. (1999) *Babe Didrikson Zaharias: The Making of a Champion*. Clarion Books.

Gotaas, T., Graves P. (2012*). Running A Global History*. United Kingdom: Reaktion Books.

Ana Guevara (2013, January 11) Sitelutions. Retrieved January 13, 2013 from:
    http://www.anagabrielaguevara.com/

Guevera Onofre, A. (2012, August 9). *London 2012 Olympics: Taiwan-Report an Olympic Land: 1960-2012*. Yahoo Voices. Retrieved from http://sports.jrank.org/

Gordon, H. (n.d.). *Betty Cuthbert*. Australian Olympic Committee. Retrieved January 2, 2012 from
    http://corporate.olympics.com.au/athlete/betty-cuthbert

Gwen Torrence. (n.d). *The New Georgia Encyclopedia*. Retrieved December 11, 1012 from
    http://www.georgiaencyclopedia.org/nge/Article.jsp?id=h-872

Joanna Hayes. Biography. (n.d.) *bio. True Story*. Retrieved December 30, 2012 from
    http://www.biography.com/people/joanna-hayes-12816734

Helen Stephens, (n.d). *Sports Reference/Olympic Sports*. Retrieved from http://www.sports-reference.com/olympics/athletes/st/helen-stephens-1.html

Helen Stephens. (n.d.). *The State Historical Society of Missouri Historic Missourians*. Retrieved from
    http://shs.umsystem.edu/historicmissourians/name/s/stephens/index.html

Hendershott, J. (1987). *Track's Greatest Women*. Los Altos, CA: Tafnews Press.

Harrington, G. (1995). *Jackie Joyner-Kersee*. New York, NY: Chelsea House.

Hill, G. (2008, October). Campbell-Brown Ends Felix's Mastery. *Track and Field News*, 40.

Hurdler Joann Hayes Poised to Make Stunning Comeback. (2012, June 22). *Associated Press*. Retrieved
    December 29, 2012 from http://www.nbcchicago.com/news/sports/Joanna-Hayes-Returns-to-Hurdles-After-Near-160064975.html

Hurdles First. (2009). Retrieved January 9, 2012 from http://hurdlesfirst.com/kimbatten.htm

Hymans, R. (2004). *The History of the U. S. Olympic Trials - Track & Field 1908-2000*. Indianapolis,
    IN: USA Track and Field.

International Association of Athletics Federation. (2009). *Brown Trafton
    Stephanie Biography*. Retrieved July, 10, 2010 from
    http://www.iaaf.org/athletes/biographies/country=USA/ athcode=183032/index.html

International Association of Athletics Federation .(n.d.). *Dragila Stacey*. Retrieved from
    http://www.iaaf.org/athletes/biographies/letter=0/athcode=110083/index.html

International Association of Athletics Federation. (n.d.). *Kara Goucher*. Retrieved August 20, 2010 from http://www.iaaf.org/athletes/biographies/letter=0/athcode=175599/index.html

International Association of Athletics Federation. (n.d.). *Sanya Richards*. Retrieved Sept 22, 2010, from http://www.iaaf.org/athletes/biographies/country=USA/ athcode=183032/index.html

Interview with Francie Larrieu Smith...an Olympic Legend. (2010, February 10). *Huxley Running Company*. Retrieved from http://huxleyrunningco.org/2012/02/10/interview-with-francie-larrieu-smith-an-olympi-legend/

Iolanda Balas. (n.d.). Retrieved December 13, 2010, from http://www.sporting-heroes.net/athletics-heroes/displayhero.asp?HeroID=7595

Joanna Hayes Foundation. (n.d.). Retrieved January 8, 2012, from http://joannahayesfoundation.org/

Joetta Sports and Beyond (2012). Retrieved Jan.13, 2012, from http://www.joettasportsandbeyond.com/

Jenkins, S. (2001). *No Finish Line, My Life As I See it*. New York, NY: G.P. Putnam's Sons.

Jews in Sports. (n.d.). Copeland, Lillian. Retrieved on December 28, 2012 from http://www.jewsinsports.org/Olympics.asp?ID=3

Joyner-Kersee, J. (1997). *A Kind of Grace: The Autobiography of the World's Greatest Female Athlete*. New York, NY: Warner Brothers Books.

Kansas Sports Hall of Fame. (2011). *Janell Smith Carson*. Retrieved December 10, 2010 from http://kshof.org/inductees/2-kansas-sports-hall-of-fame/inductees/242-smith-janell.html

Lawson, G. (1996). *World Record Breakers in Track and Field Athletics.* Champaign, IL: Human Kinetics.

Litsky, F. (2007, February 7). Willye B. White, the First 5-Time U.S. Track Olympian, Dies at 67. *The New York Times*. Retrieved from http://www.nytimes.com/2007/02/07/sports/othersports/07white.html?_r=0

Longman, J. (1996, June 10). Olympics: Run Silent, Run Fast: Torrence Takes Shots at Medals, Not Opponents. *The New York Times*. Retrieved January 8, 2012 from http://www.nytimes.com/1996/06/10/sports/olympics-run-silent-run-fast-torrence-takes-shots-at-medals-not-opponents.html?pagewanted=all&src=pm

Louis Stokes Fraser. (n.d.) *Bridgewater State University Office of Institutional Diversity*. Retrieved December 13, 2012 from http://www.bridgew.edu/HOBA/Fraser.cfm

Louis-Jacques, T. (2012, February 4). Black History Month: Louise Stokes Fraser. *Malden Patch*. Retrieved December 12, 2012 from http://malden.patch.com/groups/editors-picks/p/black-history-month-louise-stokes-fraser

MacKay, D. (2004, August 30). 50 stunning Olympic moments No 34. Kelly Holmes doubles up in Atlanta. *The Guardian*. Retrieved from http://www.guardian.co.uk/sport/blog/2012/may/29/50-stunning-olympic-moments-kelly-holmes

Malaspina, A, Velasquez, E. (2011). *Touch the Sky:Alice Coachman, Olympic High Jumper.* Park Ridge, IL: Albert Whitman and Company

Mallon, B., Buchanan, I., & Tishman, J. (1984). *Quest for Gold, The Encyclopedia of American Olympians.* New York, NY: Leisure Press.

Maraniss, D. (2008). *Rome 1960: The Olympics That Changed the World*. New York, NY: Simon & Schuster.

Marathon Woman. (n.d.). http://www.kathrineswitzer.com/index.shtml

Marin, D. & Gynn, D. (2000). *The Olympic Marathon.* Champaign, IL: Human Kinetics.

McGowan, T. (2012, August 3). Golden girl: The first Olympic speed queen. *CNN*. Retrieved December 12, 2012 from http://edition.cnn.com/2012/08/03/sport/olympics-robinson-100m-women/index.html

McGreggor, A. (1998). *Cathy Freeman; A Journey Just Begun.* Milsons Point, N.S.W.: Random House Australia.

Moore, K. (1984, August 20). Triumph and Tragedy in Los Angeles. *SI.com*. Retrieved October 2, 2010 from http://sportsillustrated.cnn.com/features/cover/2002/then_now/flashbacks/budd_082084/

Moore, K. (1992, July 22). A Long Run Gets Longer. *SI Vault.* Retrieved January 10, 2012 from http://sportsillustrated.cnn.com/vault/article/magazine/MAG1004011/2/index.htm

Murphy, F. (1992). *On A Cold, Clear Day*. Kansas City, MO: Wind Sprint Press.

National Distance Running Hall of Fame. (2010). *Doris Brown Heritage*. Retrieved August 22, 2010 from http://www.distancerunning.com/inductees/2002/heritage.html

National Distance Running Hall of Fame. (2010). *Mary Decker Slaney.* Retrieved November 10, 2010 from http://www.distancerunning.com/inductees/2003/slaney.html

Official Website of the University of Kansas Athletics Department. (n.d.). *Kansas Relays History*. Retrieved November 15, 2010 from http://www.kuathletics.com/sports/c-relay/spec-rel/relay-history.html

Olegario M Ximao, Carleton (2011). *Earlene Brown*. Ject Press

Olympic medalist Willye White dies. (2007, February 7). *USA Today*. Retrieved from
http://usatoday30.usatoday.com/sports/olympics/2007-02-07-willye-white-obit_x.htm

Official website of the Olympic Movement. (2012). http://www.olympic.org

Plowden, M. (1995). *Olympic Black Women*. Gretna, La: Pelican Publishing.

Quercetani, R.L. (2000). *Athletics - A History of Modern Track and Field Athletics (1860-2000) Men and Women*. Milan, Italy: SEP Editricesrl.

Quercetani, R.L. (2002). *Athletics - A World History of Long Distance Running (1880-2002) Men and Women*. Milan, Italy: SEP Editricesrl.

Quercetani, R.L. & Kok, N. (1992). *Athletics- A History of Modern Track and Field Athletics (1860-2000) Men and Women*. Milan, Italy: Vallardi & Associates.

Quick Facts About BettyRobinson, (2012, November 8). *Riverdale Historical Society*. Retrieved December 11, 2012 from
http://www.riverdale.lib.il.us/Community/BettyRobinson/quickfacts.html

Phelps, S. & Johnson, M. (1996). *In Contemporary Black Biography,* 13. Detroit, MI: Gale Group.

Radcliffe (2012). Retrieved Jan.11, 2013, from http://www.paularadcliffe.com/

Radcliffe, P. (2005) *Paula: My Story So Far*. UK :Simon & Schuster

Reid, R. (1997, June 15). Meet Avoids Getting Sidetracked No Controversies, Just Great Performances, Including Jearl Miles-Clarks Meet Record in the Women's 400. *Philadelphia Inquirer*. Retrieved from http://articles.philly.com/1997-06-15/sports/25528260_1_meters-kim-batten-maicel-malone

Reilly, R. (1996). She Stands Alone. *SI Vault*. Retrieved January 10, 2012 from
http://sportsillustrated.cnn.com/events/1996/olympics/storyolympic/gtorr.html

Rudolph, W. (1980). *Wilma Rudolph on Track*. New York: Wanderer Books.

Samuelson, J. (1995). *Joan Samuelson's Running for Women*. New York, NY: Rodale Press.

Sandrock, M. (1996). *Running with the Legends*. Campaign, IL: Human Kinetics.

Sears, E. (2008). *Running Through the Ages,* Jefferson, NC: McFarland.

Schwartz, L. (n.d.). Didrickson was a woman ahead of her time. *ESPN Sports Century*. Retrieved on January 3, 2013 from http://espn.go.com/sportscentury/features/00014147.html

Smith, M. (2006). *Wilma Rudolph: A Biography*. San Francisco, CA: Greenwood Press.

Spikes: The New Heroes of Athletics. (2008). *Allyson Felix*. Retrieved October 8, 2010 from
    http://www.spikesmag.com/athletes/Heroes/allysonfelix.asp

Stephanie Brown Trafton. (2011). Retrieved November 11, 2010 from http://www.stephanietrafton.com/

Switzer, K. (2009). *Marathon Woman: Running the Race to Revolutionize Women's Sports*. De Capo
    Press.

Streissguth, T. (2007). *Wilma Rudolph*, Milwaukee, WI: Turnaround Publisher.

Team USA. (2012). http://www.teamusa.org/Athletes.aspx

Track and Field News. (n.d.). Mountain View, CA: Track and Field News Press.

The Goal. (n.d.) Betty Cuthbert. Retrieved on December 23, 2012 from
    http://www.thegoal.com/players/trackfield/cuthbert_betty/cuthbert.html

Thurrock Local History Society. (n.d.). *Fatima Whitbread, M.B.E. Thurrocks's World Champion*.
    Retrieved on January 13, 2013 from http://www.thurrock-
    community.org.uk/historysoc/fatima2.htm

Tonja Buford-Bailey. (n.d.). Illinois Track and Field. Retrieved December 15, 2012 from
    http://www.fightingillini.com/sports/w-xctrack/mtt/bufordbailey_tonja00.html

Tucci, P. (2006, Dec. 6) No. 6: Lynn Jennings '83. *The Daily Princetonian*. Retrieved on January 10,
    2013 from http://www.dailyprincetonian.com/2006/12/06/16873/

Tricard, L. (2007). *American Women's Track and Field, 1981-2000: a history*. Jefferson, NC:
    MaFarland.

USA Track and Field. (n.d.). *Athlete Bios*. www.usatf.org/athletes/bios/

Valerie Brisco-Hooks Biography. (2011). Retrieved September 18, 2010 from
    http://sports.jrank.org/pages/620/Brisco-Hooks-Valerie.html.

Valmon, M. (n.d.). *Ivy Women in Sports: profiles of women from the ivy league's history- Lynn
    Jennings*. Ivy@50. Retrieved January 9, 2013 from
    http://www.ivy50.com/womens/story.aspx?sid=1/22/2007

Virginia Tech Track and Field. (n.d.). *Queen Harrison*. Retrieved October 22, 2010 from
    http://www.hokiesports.com/track/players/harrison_queen.html

Wallechinsky, D. & Loucky, J. (2008). *The Complete Book of the Olympics, 2008 Edition*. London,
    England: Aurum Press.

Whitbread, F., Blue, A. (2012) *Survivor: The Shocking and Inspiring Story of a True Champion.* United Kingdom: Virgin Books.

Whitbread, F. (2012, June 30). I Cried for a Week. *Daily Mail Online.* Retrieved January 3, 2013 from http://www.dailymail.co.uk/femail/article-2166918/Olympic-champion-Fatima-Whitbread-IVF-anguish-finally-ended-joy.html#ixzz2HfxZyTNB

About the Author

Dr. Mark Stanbrough is a professor in the Department of Health, Physical Education and Recreation at Emporia State University in Kansas. He teaches graduate and undergraduate exercise physiology and sports psychology classes and is the director of Coaching Education. The Coaching Education program at Emporia State is currently one of only ten universities in the United State to be accredited by the National Council for the Accreditation of Coaching Education. He was a co-founder of the online physical education graduate program, the first in the United States to go completely online. He received his Ph.D. in exercise physiology from the University of Oregon, and undergraduate and master's degrees from Emporia State in physical education. He has served as department chair and has served on the National Association for Sport and Physical Education National Sport Steering Committee and is a past member of the board of directors for the National Council for the Accreditation of Coaching Education.

Mark has over thirty years of coaching experience at the collegiate, high school, middle school and club level. Coach Stanbrough served eight years as the head men's and women's cross country/track and field coach at Emporia State (1984-1992) with the 1986 women's cross country team finishing second at the NAIA national meet. He has also coached at Emporia High School and Glasco High School in Kansas. He is a member of the Emporia State University Athletic Hall of Honor and the Health, Physical Education, Recreation Hall of Honor and has won numerous coach-of-the-year awards at the high school and collegiate levels.